Easy Peasy DOGGY Diary

TRAIN YOUR DOG AND TRACK THEIR PROGRESS WITH THE HELP OF THE UK'S NO.1 DOG TRAINER

STEVE MANN

BLINK
bringing you closer

First published in the UK by Blink Publishing
An imprint of Bonnier Books UK
80-81 Wimpole Street, London, W1G 9RE
Owned by Bonnier Books
Sveavägen 56, Stockholm, Sweden

facebook.com/blinkpublishing
twitter.com/blinkpublishing

Paperback – 978-1788703-54-3

A CIP catalogue of this book is available from the British Library.

Designed by Envy Design Ltd
Photographs by Dan Rouse
Illustrations by Korda Ace
Printed in Poland

1 3 5 7 9 10 8 6 4 2

This book is not intended to be a substitute for Veterinary advice. If you are
concerned that your dog has a behavioural or other disorder, you should seek
Veterinary advice. The author and publisher will not be liable for any loss or
damage in connection with or arising out of the performance or use of methods
described and contained in this book.

Every reasonable effort has been made to trace copyright holders of material
reproduced in this book, but if any have been inadvertently overlooked the
publishers would be glad to hear from them.

Blink Publishing is an imprint of Bonnier Books UK
www.bonnierbooks.co.uk

WELCOME

Ever wished you had a professional dog trainer live with you for a whole year to help with all of your training needs?

Of course you haven't, you're not mad!

Well, if I can't be your dog training lodger for 12 months, how about you take this book as a year-long 'virtual' hand-holding session, so I can coach you through loads of exciting challenges and shower you with some of my pearls of wisdom (hopefully!) garnered over the many years I've worked as a professional dog trainer.

In these pages I've shared with you my all-time favourite dog training challenges, and over the following 52 weeks you're going to visit each of the 13 challenges four times. I'm going ease you in gently the first time we lay the foundations to each challenge, but over the sessions, I've cunningly layered more and more advanced techniques so that by the end of the year, you and your best friend will be Dog Training Gurus!

You'll also discover many Easy Peasy Pearls of Wisdom to give you the inside line on projects, tasks and further adventures that you and your dog can get up to, together.

I really hope you enjoy the Diary and get as much out of it as you can, so I've added lots of areas for you to record and reflect on your training progress. After each challenge session, I've asked you a range of important Easy Peasy Ponder Points for you to consider and answer . . . honestly! Take every opportunity you can to write down your thoughts about your training, your dog and your lives together. Reflection is so important with your dog training: many a time I've sat bolt upright at 3am because I've been struck with yet another training solution. If that happens to you, then jot it down, get it out of your system and get a good night's sleep. (If you run out of space, don't shout out; just put your hand up, the teacher will be with you as soon as possible.)

I love dogs, I love training and I love people who want to do the best for their dog, so *thank you*.

When you've finished the Diary, with your thoughts and comments scrawled over the pages . . . do me a favour, keep it safe.

I *so* wish I'd kept a training diary for all the dogs I've lived with, trained and loved in the past.

You can do that now . . . enjoy.

Easy Peasy
Pearl of Wisdom:
DOG TRAINER
TALK

Us professional dog trainers, we're a funny old bunch but we love three things: dogs, wolf-print fleeces and the sound of our own voices!

You too can become the talk of the park by getting on top of the dog training vocabulary listed below, and which you'll find liberally scattered among these *Easy Peasy Doggy Diary* pages:

Cue

The cue is the signal you'll give your dog to ask for any particular behaviour. Generally, that cue will be a verbal one such as 'Sit' or 'Come', but it can also be a visual cue such as a hand in the air for *Hit the Brakes.*

Sometimes, dogs can inadvertently learn certain cues from the environment that triggers a particular behaviour. Does your dog do the behaviour of running to the door when the cue of the doorbell goes?

Priming the cue

When you give a cue, it's important to focus on what the cue **means to your dog**. As an example, when you read about teaching an Emergency Drop on page 88, for the early stages you'll *prime* that the verbal cue of 'Drop' tells your dog that treats are about to magically appear at your feet!

 4

Indication

When you and your dog get to earn your stripes as a top Detection Team on page 82, you'll read about teaching your dog an *Indication*, which is the body position your dog will do to tell you they've made a find!

Lure

To *Lure* a behaviour is to use a treat to help guide your dog into a particular position. It is a great tool to get novel behaviours up and running nice and fast. It's important that – as soon as possible – you shift from using the treat <u>before</u> the behaviour as a *Lure*, to using it <u>after</u> the behaviour, as a *Reinforcer*. If we don't make that change promptly, the dog will only do the behaviour if there is food in your hand . . . and no one wants that hassle!

Reinforcement

Reinforcement, delivered in the form of a *Reinforcer*, is anything your dog receives as a consequence of a behaviour they do, which makes that particular behaviour more like to occur again in the future. If YOU do a behaviour and as a consequence receive something wonderful, I'm pretty sure you'd love the opportunity to do that behaviour again!

You may hear the term 'positive reinforcement' in dog training. That simply means the Trainer (you!), gives something (the 'positive' part) to their dog, as a consequence of a behaviour to make that behaviour more likely to occur again in the future (the 'reinforcement' part).

Marking a behaviour

To help your dog understand WHY they got the treat after doing a fab behaviour for you, it's a valuable skill to be able to mark the behaviour. I want you to mark the behaviour with a 'Good' each time they do the behaviour you're after. You saying, 'Good' needs to be like taking a photograph the split-second your dog performs the behaviour you want them to do. Then imagine you're showing them the pic and saying, 'You see what you're doing there buddy, that's the reason you got the treat.'

Impulse Control

We've all been there in the past, channelling our inner Veruca Salt . . . 'I want it and I want it NOW!' Impulse Control is simply accepting the delay of any gratification. For you and your dog's training in this Diary, we're going to teach Impulse Control by adding Duration to your exercises. By adding a few extra seconds here and there between the behaviour being performed and the reinforcement being given, you're going to teach your dog a rare skill for any species: Patience!

WEEK 1

Boomerangs

#1

Challenge: Boomerangs #1

This exercise challenges you to be able to send your dog away to go around any object and then return back to you. Sounds tricky? It is!

Boomerangs are well worth the effort though, as once in place:

🐾 You can improve your dog's flexibility, and therefore health

🐾 You can give your dog a good physical workout without you having to keep up with the pace!

🐾 You will improve the joy of your Recalls . . . honestly!

🐾 You will add more fun to your daily walks

🐾 You will teach your dog to listen at a distance from you.

The Target: The Lure

You're going to use a treat to lure the essential movements of the Boomerang before we start building distance. Make sure your hand signal and body language are consistent as they'll become part of the set-up and cue.

For the 'object' that you are going to send your dog to go around, you can use a pole in the ground, a chair, a plant pot or a disinterested teenager.

The Training

1. With your dog on your left and a treat in your right hand, stand half a metre away from the object. Place your right foot forward and use the treat to lure your dog clockwise behind the object.

2. As soon as your dog's right shoulder passes behind the object, say, 'Good!' (to mark the behaviour), allow your dog to return to you and give them the treat. Set-up again.

3. When consistent, remove the food lure and simply cue the behaviour with your right hand.

4. Once you can smoothly lure your up-close 'baby' Boomerang, start taking a tiny step backwards as you say, 'Good' prior to reinforcing. This tiny step will help you gradually increase the distance you can successfully send your dog from. If your dog starts returning before going around the object, simply decrease your distance to a successful level.

5. When you can reliably Boomerang your dog around the object from 1 metre away, start to say, 'Boomer' as you send your dog around. Then say, 'Good' as their right shoulder passes behind the object and reinforce your dog as they return to you.

Easy Peasy Ponder Points

🐾 How many repetitions of luring did you do before you saw an 'A-ha!' moment from your dog, as they realised *A-ha! It's going around the object* (rather than just following your hand) that pays the dividends?

....

🐾 How many sessions did you do before you could Boomerang your dog from 1 metre?

....

🐾 Name 3 other objects you will use to send your dog around over the next week:

1. ....
2. ....
3. ....

🐾 Does your dog go out to, or return quicker from, the object?

....

🐾 List what happens when you throw the reinforcement behind you, rather than placing it into your dog's mouth:

....

....

🐾 What differences in your dog's performance can you note when you reinforce with a toy, rather than a treat?

....

🐾 List 5 places you can practise your baby Boomerangs this week:

1. ....
2. ....
3. ....
4. ....
5. ....

What was good?

....

....

What could be better?

....

....

What will you do to improve?

....

....

Doggy Diary

Write down all the amazing things you did with your dog this week!

Monday and Tuesday

....

....

....

Wednesday and Thursday

....

....

....

Friday

....

....

....

Saturday and Sunday

....

....

....

WEEK 2

Peek-A-Boo

#1

Challenge: Peek-A-Boo #1

On the face of it, Peek-A-Boo is a neat and impressive trick to teach your dog, but look a little deeper and it has a really solid benefit as a behaviour to ask your dog to do when you need a little more control than a standard Sit can offer, for situations such as:

🐾 Waiting in confined places such as a veterinary surgery

🐾 A great position to put your dog in for inspection and cleaning of ears, eyes and teeth

🐾 A controlled position in case you're in the company of others that aren't so confident around dogs

🐾 Securing your dog before you answer the front door to thwart an escapee!

🐾 Attaching the lead to your dog's harness

STEVE'S SECRET TOP TIP:

Treat Placement

Sometimes it doesn't really matter *where* your dog receives the treat, as long as they know *why* they got it. However, for Peek-A-Boo, it makes perfect sense to do the majority of feeding while your dog remains in the correct position. By feeding when your dog is between your legs, you're really teaching them that between your legs is a safe and very positive area to go to.

The Target: Building Confidence

Delivering Correct Body Position

Normally, when we ask our dogs to do a behaviour, we have the courtesy to look at them when we're speaking to them!

Not so much for Peek-A-Boo – instead, we want our dogs to be comfortable with two novel aspects: walking between our legs *and* approaching the back of our bodies. That's because when you think about it, those are both quite abstract concepts for our dogs to get used to.

The Training

1. To place your dog in the correct starting position, drop a treat about a couple of metres behind you for them to enjoy.

2. As they eat the treat, open your legs, bend forward and encourage your dog to place their head between your legs so you're both facing the same direction. Feed them several treats in this 'peek-a-boo' position, one at a time.

3. Throw a final treat out in front of you so they can move forward, away from you.

4. As your dog eats the thrown treat, simply turn your back to re-set for the next repetition.

Easy Peasy Ponder Points

🐾 Is your dog keen for the treats?

....

....

....

🐾 Could you feed from your two hands placed together
to keep your dog's position central?

....

....

....

🐾 Could throwing the treat further allow you more time
to re-set?

....

....

....

🐾 How often will you practise this over the next
5 days?

....

....

....

What was good?

....

....

....

....

What could be better?

....

....

....

....

What will you do to improve?

....

....

....

....

Doggy Diary

Write down all the amazing things you did with your dog this week!

Monday and Tuesday

....

....

....

Wednesday and Thursday

....

....

....

Friday

....

....

....

Saturday and Sunday

....

....

....

WEEK 3
Look To Say Please #1

Challenge: Look To Say Please #1

I've always said, if your dog's eyes aren't on you, there's a very good chance their ears aren't either! Eye contact is always one of the first exercises I teach my dogs, as it sets up the two-way channel of communication that all good relationships are built upon. Imagine talking to someone but they're not really listening . . .

I SAID, IMAGINE TALKING TO SOMEONE BUT THEY'RE NOT REALLY LISTENING . . .

When your dog looks to you, then you know:

- They're open to listening to you

- There's a very good chance you will only need to ask them once for a behaviour

- They're happy and comfortable to make a connection with you

- They've learned that you are the route to access all the good things!

- They've learned to ask nicely for something

STEVE'S SECRET TOP TIP:

Patience

Patience is one of the toughest skills to learn, eh?!
If your dog's got the necessary motivation for the
reinforcement on offer, I need you to have the
necessary patience to wait for your dog to deliver the
desired behaviour of *Eye Contact*.
Remember. . . . .
.. . .
.. . . patience. . . . .
.. . . is a virtue!

The Target: The Set-Up

At this stage, it's all about setting the scene and allowing
your dog to figure out which behaviour pays dividends.
The secret is that once you're set, stay quiet and have the
patience to allow your dog a little time for trial and error,
so they can discover the winning behaviour to offer. If the
motivation is there, then the eye contact will soon follow.
And be ready to 'mark' the behaviour with a 'Good!' the
very second it occurs, so your dog knows what behaviour to
offer again to earn more goodies.

The Training

1. Grab a handful of treats and face your dog. With the treats in your closed fist, hold your hand at arm's length away from your body.

2. Say nothing. Let your dog investigate your treat-filled but closed fist. They'll paw, they'll sniff, they'll lick . . . but you still say nothing. Once they've tried all of the obvious, they'll glance towards you and as soon as they do that . . . BOOM! You say, 'Good!', give them a fuss and give them a treat then. By you saying, 'Good!' to 'mark' the Eye Contact as soon as it happens, your dog will have a good clue about what is the go-to behaviour to offer next time.

2. Once your dog finishes their treat, place your treat-filled fist out to the side again for several more successful repetitions.

Easy Peasy Ponder Points

🐾 Are you staying nice and quiet to allow your dog to figure out how to get the treats?

....

....

....

🐾 What treats get you the best motivation?

....

....

....

🐾 What evidence of learning can you see?

....

....

....

🐾 Where else could you sit that is quieter?

....

....

....

What was good?

....

....

....

....

What could be better?

....

....

....

....

What will you do to improve?

....

....

....

....

Doggy Diary

Write down all the amazing things you did with your dog this week!

Monday and Tuesday

....

....

....

Wednesday and Thursday

....

....

....

Friday

....

....

....

Saturday and Sunday

....

....

....

WEEK 4

Supersonic Sits #1

Challenge: Supersonic Sits #1

I'm going to level with you here. I've made a career out of teaching thousands of professional dog trainers as many different exercises as possible, but if your dog can do a good old 'common-or-garden' Sit when you ask them to, you're going to help them avoid 99% of the potential problems dogs typically get into. Let's be honest, why look for complicated when simple will do!

The basics of Sit are nice and easy at an entry level, but we're going to teach it to a university-degree level, so you've got a rock-solid, reliable behaviour, no matter what else is going on.

- Dog jumps up to greet visitors? Ask them to Sit to say, 'Hello'

- Dog running towards an unknown dog? Ask them to Sit, so you can assess the situation before it's too late

- Dog eyeing up the child with the ice cream? Ask them to Sit, quickly!

- Tricky to pop the lead back on to your dog after an off-lead play? Ask them to Sit

STEVE'S SECRET TOP TIP:

Proofing

Any eejit (including me!) can get their dog to Sit nicely when they're holding their food bowl next to the fridge in the kitchen, but the real skill and benefit of the exercise is to make it as reliable as possible *no matter where you are or what else is going on*. That's where *proofing* comes in. *Proofing* a behaviour means we're going to teach it in many different environments with a variety of set-ups, so the behaviour of Sit can be as robust and reliable as possible.

The Target: The Solid Foundation

Even if you've taught your dog to Sit in the past, and let's be honest, who hasn't, I want us all to start here so we can build a super-strong foundation which will enable us to accelerate though the trickier stages as we progress. See it as a refresher course, a bit like going back to infant school and sitting on those tiny little chairs again.

The Training

1. Hold a treat to your dog's nose in your right hand. Once they sniff the treat, slowly raise your hand up and slightly over your dog's head. As they shift their weight backwards and their butt touches the floor, say, 'Good', and pop the treat into their mouth as they Sit. Once done, give them a fuss to get them out of position, so that you then reload and repeat the above 5 times. (Warning! Don't be tempted to say, 'Sit' yet, this comes later, be patient!)

2. As above in stage 1 but to *proof* the behaviour, have the treat in your *left* hand. It's important to practise from a variety of angles and set-ups, so that no matter what the situation, when you say, 'Sit', your dog will sit. Repeat 5 times.

3. Now the behaviour has become nice and reliable, it's time to add the verbal cue by saying, 'Sit' as your dog shifts their weight backwards and plants their butt on the floor. Make sure you say, 'Good' as soon as they assume the position . . . and pay well!

4. Now time to mix it up. Sometimes lure with your left hand, sometimes with your right. Say, 'Sit' just before you raise your treat-laden hand to get the behaviour.

5. Now with no treats in your hand, using just the hand signal and the verbal cue, ask your dog to 'Sit' and pay well with a treat from your pouch when they do.

6. Try a few with the emphasis on your verbal cue. After each successful repetition, reduce the length of your hand signal by 20% until your dog will sit with the verbal cue only.

Easy Peasy Ponder Points

🐾 How's your timing? Make sure you're saying, 'Good'
the *split-second* your dog's butt touches the floor.

....

🐾 Are you going too far too soon? If any element seems
a little tricky for your dog, just go back a few steps to
build up confidence, and take tiny steps towards the
next stage.

....

🐾 Is the surface comfortable for your dog to sit on?

....

🐾 Are you ready to proof even further by practising in different locations?

....

🐾 Could you practise different times of day? Inside? Outside? Night time?

....

What was good?

....

....

....

What could be better?

....

....

....

What will you do to improve?

....

....

....

Easy Peasy
Pearl of Wisdom:
WINTER

I love wintertime with my dogs now, but as a young, dog-training apprentice, I often had to have the mantra of, *'There's no such thing as bad weather, only bad clothing . . . OR BAD ATTITUDE!'* drilled into me many-a-time by an older dog trainer out in the tundra.

Although a 'bit of rain' or a 'tad chilly' is no excuse not to take your dog out for a play to blow away the cobwebs, in extreme weather, we really need to make sure we're looking after our dogs, especially if you're the proud owner of:

- A breed with a fine coat such as a Greyhound, Whippet, Staffordshire Bull Terrier or Boxer.

- A small breed of dog with a low 'under-carriage' close to the cold wet ground such as a Dachshund or Corgi.

- An elderly dog or one prone to illness.

- A puppy.

As winter draws in, so do the shorter days and it's easy to be caught out with your dog as the daylight disappears. Ensure you remain highly visible to traffic and avoid scaring the bejaysus out of other walkers by having your dog wear a flashing light on their collar. Always carry an emergency torch and both of you should wear reflective clothing. In snowy weather, your dog may pick up grit or salt on their feet. Wash them thoroughly to avoid irritation and, importantly, to avoid your dog 'self-grooming' and ingesting any nasties.

Stay on top of hairy toes by trimming any long hairs on the feet. Hair between the toes has a nasty habit of collecting snow, which in turn forms into little ice balls that can painfully lodge between the digits. (Also, please check out our 'Grooming' Pearl of Wisdom on page 170 as keeping your dog's coat in tip-top condition throughout winter will make sure its protection and insulation qualities are at their best.)

Be super careful if you usually let your dog off-lead for a gallop. During the wintertime, snow may make everything look, and smell, slightly different so if you lose track of each other, it could make navigation more difficult than usual for your dog to relocate you. In addition, please be belt-and-braces with your vigilance if you have any rivers or lakes on your walks during winter. Freezing water can inflict hypothermia horribly fast and frozen water can give a false sense of security.

Keep an eye on your dog's weight. Not too closely, don't make them paranoid, but cold weather can play havoc with one's weight – just look at Santa! Some dogs may burn more calories in the cold weather, some may burn less due to limited physical exercise opportunities during 'indoor-playtime' weather. Just observe and adjust feed accordingly.

Finally, if your dog may benefit from wearing a coat when the weather's inclement, go ahead and kit them out as you see fit. Don't listen to any plum who says, 'Dogs don't need coats, they never used to wear them in the wild.' Just smile and reply, 'Neither did humans, darling.' (At this point, I like to toss back my hair and flamboyantly flick up my heels as I walk on, but it's up to you.)

With all that being said, sharing a bracing walk with your dog in the wintertime and then getting cosy indoors as the pair of you curl up together is, basically, the best! Just remember, please, err on the side of caution and look after the pair of you – summer will soon be here!

TRAINING

IS PLAY

AND

PLAY IS

TRAINING

WEEK 5
The Magic Hand
Touch #1

Challenge: The Magic Hand Touch #1

Tell no one, but this exercise not only looks good and has tons of useful applications, it's also bloomin' easy to teach! In addition to being a great tool to teach pups and younger dogs, it's also a lovely, gentle way to give your older dog a little workout and mental exercise, without them having to do too many Sits and Downs with creaking joints. Old age catches up on all of us eventually!

If you can harness the dog training holy trinity of *motivation*, *patience* and *timing*, then as soon as you have a decent Hand Touch in your locker, you'll have:

- A great way to introduce your dog to friends who may not be too confident around dogs

- A positive way to keep your dog stationary for vet inspections and grooming

- 'Power-steering' to guide your dog from danger

- A way to show your dog that human hands coming towards them are good news

- A technique to help you pop the lead back onto their harness after a run-around

STEVE'S SECRET TOP TIP:

The Flourish

Offering your hand for your dog to touch with their nose is a window of opportunity for them to get the reinforcement they crave. The sight of your hand being produced is the cue, so make sure you deliver it with a flamboyant *flourish* to create a unique cue, but also to garner your dog's curiosity and to encourage a positive nose-to-hand interaction.

The Target: The Lure

You're going to introduce your hand signal for the Hand Touch by initially using a lure between your fingers to get the behaviour, BUT you're going to reinforce with a different treat from your other hand to stop your dog getting too fixated on the initial lure. We don't want your dog to only do the behaviour if they're fixated on the treat in your hand.

The Training

1. Place a treat between the middle two fingers of your right hand and hold that hand behind your back.

2. With your dog facing you, FLOURISH your right hand from behind your back like an auditioning magician and have your palm facing your dog, 30 centimetres from their nose.

3. As soon as your dog touches their nose onto your hand, say, 'Good', put your 'lure' hand back behind your back and give your dog a treat from your treat pouch or pocket with your left hand.

4. Repeat several times then swap hands so that your left hand now holds the treat and your right hand gives the reinforcement.

5. Finally, flourish your hand *with no treat* between your fingers. As your dog touches their nose to your palm, as before, say, 'Good' (to mark the behaviour), remove the target hand and reinforce with a treat from your other hand.

Easy Peasy Ponder Points

🐾 What future applications do you think you can use your Hand Touch for in real life?

....

🐾 Can you think of two reasons why it's better to 'Hand Touch' your dog from danger as opposed to pulling on the lead?

....

....

🐾 Which treats work best for you for this exercise?

....

🐾 Does your dog find this easier from a sitting, standing or lying position?

....

🐾 What happens if you hold your Lure Hand further from your dog's nose?

....

🐾 What evidence of learning can you see?

....

What was good?

....

....

....

....

What could be better?

....

....

....

....

What will you do to improve?

....

....

....

....

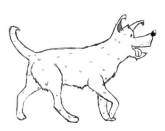

Doggy Diary

Write down all the amazing things you did with your dog this week!

Monday and Tuesday

....

....

....

Wednesday and Thursday

....

....

....

Friday

....

....

....

Saturday and Sunday

....

....

....

WEEK 6
The Smiling Lead
#1

Challenge: The Smiling Lead #1

Loose-lead walking, eh? Or as I prefer to call it, The Smiling Lead . . .

Hands up who's had difficulty mastering this bad boy to date! Walking your dog on the lead is probably the exercise you've done the most of, the issue you've tried the hardest to crack, yet still the Holy Grail of walking more than 10 steps with a loose lead defies you!

Don't worry, I've got a plan!

When you can walk your dog on a loose lead:

- Walks will be so much more comfortable for both of you

- Icy paths won't be the perilous threat they previously were!

- You'll reduce frustration on the lead (both ends!)

- Your dog won't feel the physical pain of restraint

- Your arms will remain the same length!

STEVE'S SECRET TOP TIP:
Discipline

The Smiling Lead is one of the simplest, yet most difficult things you can teach your dog!

Simple because it hinges on us reinforcing just the one core behaviour.

Difficult because the one ingredient that is always essential from us as handlers is often missing: discipline.

I understand that sometimes you'll need to get your dog walk over and done ASAP. You don't have time for *training*. But here's the deal: when just don't have the time or headspace for training and you need to get from A to B as quickly as you can, pop a different harness onto your dog and tie a bandana around their neck. When they're in their *pulling* harness and are wearing their bandana, they're allowed to pull; you're not allowed to stop them! (I much prefer popping the lead onto a harness as opposed to a collar as it prevents stress being put on the dog's neck.)

When you DO have your training-head on and you're focused, walk them in their proper loose-lead walking harness with no bandana. That way, you won't be sending mixed messages and corrupting your training. Your dog will also no longer have the embarrassment of sporting his neckerchief, like a hairy Albert Steptoe.

The Target: Stationary Checking-In

If your dog is regularly giving you Eye Contact on their walk, then they can't pull you on-lead at the same time. Therefore, Eye Contact is going to be our *core behaviour* for our Smiling Lead.

The exercise that follows will teach your dog that it's in their interest to look at you. First, *stationary* as per below, then *on the move* as our training progresses.

The Training

1. With your dog wearing the harness you want them to wear in the future when they're walking on-lead nicely, pop the lead on and stand upright. Without saying a word, drop a treat onto the floor for your dog to enjoy, count 5 seconds, drop a treat again, and again, and again.

2. After several treat drops, your dog will begin to anticipate the next one falling for them. When the next one doesn't automatically appear for them, they'll look up to where the previous treats fell from in order to say, 'Oi. Where's my treats?!' AS SOON AS they glance up to you, say, 'Good!' (to mark the behaviour) and drop the next treat.

3. Continue to say, 'Good!' and drop a treat each time they look up to you. You're now reinforcing Eye Contact. I told you it was simple, didn't I?

(Don't worry, the difficult bit comes in a later week!)

Easy Peasy Ponder Points

🐾 Timing. Are you teaching as effectively as possible by saying, 'Good?' the *split second* your dog looks to you?

....

....

🐾 Are you standing upright? Let's consistently practise the final body position we'll be in when we're walking on-lead for real.

....

....

🐾 Has your dog realised it's their Eye Contact to you that makes the food appear? If you suspect not, make sure the treats remain in your pocket or treat pouch *until* you say, 'Good!'

....

....

🐾 Is your training environment nice and quiet, or could you move somewhere less distracting?

....

....

What was good?

....

....

....

....

What could be better?

....

....

....

....

What will you do to improve?

....

....

....

....

Doggy Diary

Write down all the amazing things you did with your dog this week!

Monday and Tuesday

....

....

....

Wednesday and Thursday

....

....

....

Friday

....

....

....

Saturday and Sunday

....

....

....

WEEK 7
The Seek Back
#1

Challenge: The Seek Back #1

Seek Backs are a simple way to engage the most complex tools that your dog possesses: their nose and their brain!

This exercise is ideal for dogs of all ages and it can be performed on or off the lead for safety. Once you've laid the fundamental foundations of a Seek Back, you'll be able to:

- Enjoy more attention and fun on your daily walks

- Make mealtimes more interesting

- Engage your dog's nose for extra mental release

- Lead a game that your dog will be an absolute expert at!

- Go 'hunting' together with your dog, as a team

The Target: Seek Back Foundations

Here, we're going to introduce all of the essential foundations of a Seek Back and get those ideas in place solidly, before we evolve towards adding a little creativity later.

The Training

1. With your dog on-lead to your left-hand side and your treat pouch held in your right hand, start walking forward together.

2. After several steps, when your dog isn't looking, sneakily drop your treat pouch to the floor. Don't break your stride, just innocently continue walking forward with your dog.

3. After a further 5–10 steps, excitedly say to your dog, 'Where's it gone?' As your dog looks up to you, drop your right hand down to your dog's nose level to guide them as you both do an about-turn to face the direction you've just come from. Say, 'Find It!' and together start urgently looking for the dropped treat pouch.

4. As soon as your dog stumbles upon the pouch, have a HUGE celebration, fall to your knees and bring out a few treats individually from your pouch for your dog to enjoy.

Easy Peasy Ponder Points

🐾 It's not the end of the world if your dog sees you drop your treat pouch but be honest, if you did 10 repetitions, how many times can you drop the treat pouch without your dog noticing?

....

🐾 How many sessions did you do before your dog realised that 'Find it!' meant there was something out there for them to search for?

....

🐾 What body language do you see from your dog when they hit upon the scent of the treat pouch?

....

🐾 List 5 other things your dog loves that you're going to drop instead of the treat pouch as you continue to practise this week?

1. ....
2. ....
3. ....
4. ....
5. ....

What was good?

....

....

....

....

What could be better?

....

....

....

....

What will you do to improve?

....

....

....

....

Doggy Diary

Write down all the amazing things you did
with your dog this week!

Monday and Tuesday

....

....

....

Wednesday and Thursday

....

....

....

Friday

....

....

....

Saturday and Sunday

....

....

....

WEEK 8

Total Recalls

#1

Challenge: Total Recalls #1

Considering the sheer volume of times you're going to call your dog to you in their lifetime, teaching a brilliant Recall is surely the best use of your time you could ever spend! A small investment of your time now could save you a HUUUUUGE amount of time later as you desperately beg for your dog to PLEEEEASE come back, for the hundredth time, on your hands and knees, crying. In the dark. Raining.

Simply put, the better your dog's Recall, the better your life together can be.

No matter how good (or bad) your dog's Recall is at the moment, let's work together NOW to make improvements. By being able to allow your dog responsible off-lead time, the pair of you are going to be able to afford:

🐾 **More** opportunity for exploration during walks

🐾 **More** comfort for you, so you can go hands-free!

🐾 **More** opportunity for your dog to run around, making the most of their walks through physical and mental release

🐾 **More** peace of mind knowing that, if needs be, you can call your dog back to you for safety

STEVE'S SECRET TOP TIP:
Reflex-Like Reactions

Nothing's more important than a reliable Recall, so I don't want your dog to have to slowly ponder, weighing up the pros and cons with their doggy pals before deciding whether to run to you or not when you call. I want your dog's Recall to be like an instant REFLEX! To get that reflex, you're going to double-down on giving your Recall cue a really positive association.

The Target: Making the Association

Building the Reflex

The British Olympic sprint legend Linford Christie famously stated that he always aimed to go on the B of the BANG!, in other words the very split-second the starter pistol fired. That's what I want your dog to do – to start their run-back to you on the C of the 'COME!' To get to that level of reflex reaction, we need to focus on this question: *'What do we want the sound of 'COME!' to mean to your dog?'*

So here we go. Grab your dog, your treats, 5 minutes and let's do this.

The Training

1. Stand by your dog, but remain silent, totally passive like you're stood at a bus stop. All of a sudden, out of the blue shout 'COME!' and then excitedly produce several treats for your dog to scoff. If they're nuts about a particular toy, now's the time to produce it and have a frenzied joy-filled play for 10 seconds then STOP! Stand silent again.

2. Your dog will look at you like you've just shown them a card trick, bemused yet entertained! I want you to remain silent for a minute longer as it's that silence that will give your dog a chance to *consider and download* what just happened. When you're ready . . . GO! Shout 'COME!' and immediately make like a party for 10–15 seconds – shower your dog with whatever they adore for 15 seconds of mayhem then . . . again . . . FREEZE!

3. Repeat 5–10 times per session and soon enough your dog will start looking to you as if to say, 'Go on, give us a Recall, being next to you once you've said, "COME!" is the best fun ever!'

4. Once you can see your dog eyeing you up to try and hypnotise you into saying, 'COME!', then I want you to practise the same in as many different locations as possible to make the Reflex as robust as possible. The location may be different but the common denominator remains the same: 'COME!' *means good times with you.*

Easy Peasy Ponder Points

🐾 Are you making sure you say, 'COME!' and THEN producing the treats or toys? It's important that the treats and toys aren't in sight *until you say, 'COME!'*. We want the Recall to **predict** the appearance of the good stuff.

....

....

🐾 To make the Recall association as strong and reliable as possible, are you delivering the treats and fun *within 1 second* of saying, 'COME!'? Any longer and the association may be lost. This is where your Ninja-like timing and speed come into play!

....

....

🐾 Are you using the very best reward for your dog? Try a few and use what your dog loves the most. Don't produce a bronze medal when you could have a gold one in your back pocket!

....

....

Are you nice and passive between Recall parties? The more contrast you can put between each repetition, the clearer the message will be to your dog that it's 'COME!' that makes the good times roll.

....

What was good?

....

....

....

What could be better?

....

....

....

What will you do to improve?

....

....

....

Easy Peasy
Pearl of Wisdom:
STEVE'S TOP 6
EASY PEASY DOG
TRAINING TIPS

T ake some advice from an old fool. I've made all the mistakes there are to make with dogs and training, and it took me years to figure this lot out!

1. Your dog won't always remember what you told them to DO, but they'll always remember how you make them FEEL

This may sound odd coming from a professional dog trainer, but don't take your training too seriously. Chip away a little at a time and remember: if your dog wants to hang around with you because you're fun to be with, you're 90% there already! Give me a happy dog with room to improve over an obedient dog with a heavy heart.

2. Your dog is *always* right

Oh, this can be a hard one to accept, but tough: suck it up, buttercup! Your dog always makes what they believe is the right decision, given the information they have to hand. If you say, 'Come!', they'll immediately run a risk/benefit analysis:

If I do a Recall now, history suggests I'll get something AWESOME ☺ *or. . . If I do a Recall now, history suggests I'll just be put on the lead and all my fun will be OVER* ☹ *or. . . If I don't do a Recall, I can run over to flirt with the poodle, roll in the fox poo AND stay away from the lead!* ☺☺☺

Not only is your dog always right – They Can Never Be Wrong! Your dog will never be *wrong* or make *mistakes*. They will merely give you *feedback*. You didn't hit the criteria you were aiming at? No biggie, lower your criteria, check that the environment is not too distracting and go again. Hit your target, celebrate success together and continue to build an optimistic dog.

Oscar Wilde said that, 'Experience is simply the name we give mistakes.' However, he was a shocking dog trainer. I'd say that mistakes are simply the name that we to give *feedback*.

Your dog will always make the right decision as far as they're concerned. Your job is twofold: first, build up a history and faith that when they do what you ask them to, it leads to greatness; secondly, don't let them be reinforced for inappropriate behaviours by using my third tip.

3. Control & Management

Of course, we want your dog to receive plenty of reinforcement for doing the appropriate behaviours you like, so they can do them again. What we DON'T want is your dog being reinforced for doing the *inappropriate behaviours* you DON'T like!

Good training is obviously the answer but training is a process, not an event. It takes time to spin the wheels before you get any traction, and sometimes you need a quick solution NOW.

That's where Control & Management comes in.

🐾 **Your dog doesn't YET have a good Recall?**
No problem, attach a long line to their harness so they can't run off and get into danger.

🐾 **You dog hasn't YET learned not to jump up onto visitors at the door?**
No problem, pop your dog in the kitchen or garden before you open the front door.

🐾 **You dog hasn't YET learned to walk past the dog at Number 53 when you turn left from your house to go for your walk?**
Cool. Turn right.

If your dog doesn't Recall to you but runs off and has a lovely time running with other dogs, or if they adore the fuss the visitor gives them as they jump at them by the front door, or they receive a chemical brain-bath of excitement when they bark at their nemesis at Number 53, *they're being reinforced for the behaviours you don't want them to be reinforced for.*

Control & Management. It's not very glamorous, but it's definitely the unsung hero of dog training.

4. DON'T aim for the moon and (pretend you'd) be happy with the stars

Set small, wafer-thin targets in your training and, most importantly, celebrate them with your dog when you achieve them. If you set tough goals then you may never be able to 'finish on a high' as the dog-training cliché goes. (I was once up till 4am, complete with head-lamp, trying to finish on a 'high'. My dog hated me!)

If you set small targets and achieve them, you'll BOTH get a little boost of reinforcement. You know what that reinforcement will do? It'll inspire you to set, then tick off the next wafer-thin increase in criteria. Then the next . . . then the next . . . before you know it, you'll be writing a book!

5. PLAY is training, and training is play

I never want your dog to differentiate between Play and Training. It should always feel like a privilege and a game for both of you. It should feel that way for you too.

6. Reflect: What valuable lessons could YOU learn from your dog?

....

....

WEEK 9
Detection Dog
#1

Challenge: Detection Dog #1

Your dog's amazing ability to sniff out scents is a superhero skill that the likes of you and I can only dream of having. I've travelled the world working with Detection Dogs, from wildlife-tracking dogs in Africa to drug dogs in the UK: when it comes to following their nose, dogs absolutely smash it!

By working with your dog to tap into their scent-detection prowess, you're going to create an amazing pastime that you can enjoy together as a team, plus you'll be constructively providing plenty of mental exercise for them so they can relax contentedly of an evening, safe in the knowledge of a job well done!

By working through our Easy Peasy Scent Detection Challenge, you will:

- Tap into your dog's natural instincts

- Learn more about your dog and their scenting ability and refine your skills as a dog trainer

- Share the joy of searching as a pastime with your dog

- Learn a fun and constructive method to *exercise* your dog, even if injured, very young or very old

- Teach them to target a specific scent, like a true working Detection Dog

STEVE'S SECRET TOP TIP:

Preparation!

As your Scent-Detection training develops, you're going to be *handling* and hiding a target odour, such as clove oil, gun oil or birch oil. It's important you prepare these 'hides' like a pro. That means:

DON'T GET IT ALL OVER YOUR HANDS!

Handle the Target Scent jar and cotton wool balls like they're volatile dynamite. The only target scent in the area needs to be where you've deliberately hidden it. This means:

- Wear gloves
- Use tweezers
- Be a Scent-Detection training pro!

The Target: Introducing the Detection Game

I need you to source a couple of small pots for me. Perhaps old camera film cases or some empty make-up pots. Give them a good clean out and drill a couple of holes in the lid of each. We're going to use these pots to teach what is known as 'scent discrimination' and also to introduce your dog to the fact that sniffing in the right area pays well!

The Training

1. Just take one pot for now, load it with treats, pop the lid on, sit in your chair and hold the pot behind your back. Have your dog in front of you, between your legs as you sit.

2. Say, 'Find It' and *immediately* hold the pot out in front of you for your dog to sniff. As soon as they sniff the pot, say, 'Good!' (to mark the behaviour), unscrew the lid and give them a treat. Praise them well! The act of sniffing the correct pot is known as 'the Indication'.

Repeat the process several times until your dog can't wait to pop their nose on the lid as soon as you say, 'Find It' when you present the pot.

3. Now have two pots behind your back, one loaded with treats, one empty. Say, 'Find It' and present both pots out in front of you for your dog to investigate. When they sniff the empty pot, say nothing, be patient. When they sniff the loaded pot, as before, say, 'Good', unscrew the lid and give them their wages!

When they're showing more interest in the loaded pot over the empty one, you've started the *scent-discrimination* process. Go you!

4. After several repetitions, to build duration of the Indication, allow your dog to sniff the loaded pot a few seconds longer each time before saying, 'Good'.

Easy Peasy Ponder Points

🐾 Are you saying, 'Find It' a split-second prior to producing the pots?

....

🐾 Could you vary the way you produce the two pots? Wider apart? One in front of the other? One high, one low?

....

🐾 Are you sure you're saying, 'Good' as your dog *sniffs* the target pot?

....

🐾 Are you being too greedy, trying to build the duration of the Indication too soon?

....

🐾 How can you be sure your dog's not just guessing?!

....

What was good?

....

....

....

....

What could be better?

....

....

....

....

What will you do to improve?

....

....

....

....

Doggy Diary

Write down all the amazing things you did with your dog this week!

Monday and Tuesday

....

....

....

Wednesday and Thursday

....

....

....

Friday

....

....

....

Saturday and Sunday

....

....

....

WEEK 10

The Emergency

Drop #1

Challenge: The Emergency Drop #1

What if somehow you've knocked your bread knife off your kitchen counter only for your dog to enthusiastically pick it up? Now what? That's where your Emergency Drop is going to be a life-saver.

The method I'm going to teach you is one I've used hundreds of times over many years to teach security dogs to let go of 'bad guys', eventually! ☺

Having your dog 'Drop' an item when you ask them to is going to:

- Make playing with toys more fun for both of you

- Give you peace of mind if you're clumsy in the kitchen

- Allow your dog to trust that you won't *steal* from them

- Stop you having to wrestle stinky, rotten rabbit carcasses from your dog's jaws!

STEVE'S SECRET TOP TIP:
Priming

I'm going to help you to **prime** the value of the cue. First by associating the 'Drop' verbal cue with the treats your dog wants. Once the association has been made, you'll then be able to confidently use the cue of 'Drop' to get the behaviour YOU want. It's a win–win!

The Target: Priming the Cue

The good news for your dog here is that – unusually and cunningly – you're going to use TWO treats each time you give the cue 'Drop'. First, you'll put a treat by your feet so that your dog's attention shoots to you, but crucially you'll then follow-up with a second, thrown, treat which will stop you having to dash back to pick up a dangerous dropped item before your dog beats you to it!

The first step towards this very important exercise is to teach your dog that whenever they hear you say, 'Drop', they should literally drop everything and bolt to you.

The Training

1. Wander around the room or your garden, ignoring your dog for a few silent moments . . . suddenly, out of the blue, shout, 'Drop!' and *then* place a tasty treat by your feet for your dog to run to and grab. *As soon as they've eaten the first treat,* say, 'Good' and throw the second treat 5 metres away for your dog to chase and eat.

In future, the anticipation of the second treat immediately following treat 1 will prevent your dog from rushing back to the dropped item you don't want in their mouths.

2. Repeat the above step several times in a variety of locations to really ingrain the fact that as soon as your dog hears the cue, 'Drop', they can't help but race to you in anticipation of good times!

Easy Peasy Ponder Points

🐾 How many repetitions did you do before you saw a reflex-like reaction to the sound of 'Drop'?

....

🐾 List 5 new areas you can practise your 'Drop' cue priming:

1. ....

2. ....

3. ....

4. ....

5. ....

🐾 Are you saying, 'Drop' with the same tone, volume and urgency you would if there was a real-life emergency? Remember, this might save your dog's life . . .

....

🐾 Who else do you know that should *prime* the cue 'Drop' for your dog?

....

🐾 Try 5 different treats. List in order of today's preference:

1. ....

2. ....

3. ....

4. ....

5. ....

🐾 Does your dog's treat preference change from one day to the next?

....

What was good?

....
....
....

What could be better?

....
....
....

What will you do to improve?

....
....
....

Doggy Diary

Write down all the amazing things you did with your dog this week!

Monday and Tuesday

....

....

....

Wednesday and Thursday

....

....

....

Friday

....

....

....

Saturday and Sunday

....

....

....

WEEK 11
Hit The Brakes
#1

Challenge: Hit The Brakes #1

Once, when I was only 15 I ran into an off-licence to try and score some beers for my mates. As I hastily bowled up to the counter, all brave-like, who should I see with their back to me but my school's headteacher. THAT'S how hard I want your dog to Hit the Brakes when you ask them to stop!

When you teach your dog to Hit the Brakes (and I insist you do!), you'll have:

🐾 A genuine potential life-saving exercise up your sleeve

🐾 Skills to blow the socks off the local dog whisperer

🐾 The concept of 'Distance Control' in your training portfolio, so your dog will learn that the opportunity to earn rewards doesn't just happen when they're next to you

'A potential life-saver' is not overestimating the importance of Hit the Brakes. I've had owners in the past thank me for teaching them Hit the Brakes, which they had to put to good use when their dog had squeezed out of their front door, crossed the road and was just about to run back over the road straight into oncoming traffic. A Recall wouldn't have helped; it was Hit the Brakes that saved that dog's life that day. (The next class they attended, I got cake!)

STEVE'S SECRET TOP TIP:
Consistency

Once you're up and running with Hit the Brakes, you're going to be asking your dog for the behaviour in a variety of scenarios: sometimes they'll be running towards you; sometimes they'll be running away from you; sometimes you'll be stationary; sometimes, no doubt, *you'll* be running!

The one thing I want to rely on you to do is to be *consistent* with the way you ask your dog for the behaviour. No matter what else is happening, I want you to always use the same hand, the same tone, the same volume and for you to make the same silhouette when you cue Hit the Brakes (when your dog is a distance away from you, not only are you using your voice to ask for Hit the Brakes, but you're also cueing the behaviour with your body position). So, I'm going to teach you to <u>always</u> cue the behaviour with your hand **above** your head, to offer a nice clear silhouette for your dog to learn from. A hand *in front* of your body will be visually lost by your dog once they're a certain distance from you; an arm above the head will always be clear.

Traditionally, most dog training focuses on getting your dog closer and nearer to you. Hit the Brakes makes a refreshing change from that template because it's about teaching and having control over your dog, even though they're a distance away from you. Now there's a super power!

The Target: 'Charging Up' the 'Hit the Brakes' Cue

As always, when you give your dog a cue to do behaviour, I want you to ask yourself, *What does it mean to my dog?*

Simply put, at this stage, when you say, 'Stop!' to your dog, it's gonna mean that a treat's about to land behind their butt. Nothing more, nothing less!

So, for the exercise below – and I know it's an odd one but I want you to trust me – when you say, 'Stop!', your dog's going to get a treat *regardless* of their behaviour.

I know, crazy, right?

What we're doing is 'charging up' the value of the cue. Once we've done that, we can then shift on to reinforcing the actual behaviour, but, first things first . . .

The Training

1. Place 5 treats on the floor for your dog to keep them occupied so you can sneak away 4 or 5 metres.

2. Stand sideways on to them, have a treat ready in your hand and as soon as they look up from finishing their treats, raise the arm nearest your dog in the air, say, 'Stop!' as you move your hand similar to a police officer stopping traffic; then with the second movement of your hand, throw the treat to land behind your dog's butt, **regardless** of what your dog does.

3. Your dog will dash off their treat and, as soon as they do, be ready! The moment their head comes up from eating the treats, you're there: consistent body language, sideways on, treat in hand, raised arm say, 'Stop!' on the first beat then on the second beat, throw the treat to land behind your dog's butt.

4. Repeat 10 times to really key in the fact that when you say, 'Stop!', a treat <u>will</u> land behind your dog's butt.

5. Once your dog puts two and two together when they see your policeman body language and hear the cue, 'Stop!', what are they going to do in anticipation of a treat about to land behind their butt?

That's it, STOP!

Clever, eh?

Easy Peasy Ponder Points

Could your throwing be more accurate? If so, pop your dog away, grab 10 treats, place a bin 10 metres away from you . . . and practise!

....

Would a long line trailing on the floor behind your dog make the set-up safer?

....

🐾 Are your treats easy for your dog to find? Use treats that are large enough and contrast in colour to the ground to ensure you don't waste time turning the session into a searching game.

....

🐾 Is your body language, volume and tone consistent?

....

🐾 Are you making a nice clear silhouette for your dog to learn from, with your arm clearly over your head?

....

What was good?

....

....

What could be better?

....

....

What will you do to improve?

....

....

Doggy Diary

Write down all the amazing things you did with your dog this week!

Monday and Tuesday

....

....

....

Wednesday and Thursday

....

....

....

Friday

....

....

....

Saturday and Sunday

....

....

....

WEEK 12

Say Your Prayers

#1

Challenge: Say Your Prayers #1

Not only is 'Say Your Prayers' the cutest trick in the world, but when performed correctly it also serves as an excellent movement to help your dog stretch and maintain a balanced core mobility.

Once you have this technique in your box of tricks you will:

- Be able to help your dog maintain flexibility in their shoulders and spine
- Never fail to impress friends and family
- Scoop first prize at the local talent show!

STEVE'S SECRET TOP TIP:

Kit

A bad workman always blames his tools – but not us! For this exercise, you are going to need a platform that has a surface height somewhere between your dog's elbow and shoulder. Depending on the size of your dog, the right platform may be a chair, a footstool or for the diddy dogs like my Chihuahua, a thick book! Too high and it'll be too much of a stretch for your dog. Too low and we won't be able to stop your dog slipping into a Down or Bow position.

The Target: Introduce The Platform

Every journey starts with one step, so we're going to use a lure to encourage your dog to target their foot onto your chosen platform. Once they realise that putting their foot on the platform gets rewarded, then the rest will follow.

The Training

1. Allow your dog to investigate the platform, then with you on one side of the platform and your dog on the other, lure their head over the platform with a treat and then feed in that position.

2. Once your dog is comfortably taking the treats with their head over the platform, draw your hand back a little further to encourage your dog to stretch towards you, over the platform, to take the treat.

3. With a treat in your hand, lure your dog further towards you and as soon as they place a foot onto the platform say, 'Good' and feed several individual treats as they remain in position.

Easy Peasy Ponder Points

🐾 Experiment with 5 different treats. List in order of preference:

1. ....

2. ....

3. ....

4. ....

5. ....

When it's time to lure a foot onto the platform, is the exercise smoother if you raise the treat slightly higher?

....

....

Is your dog more likely to remain on the platform if you move slower or faster to treat?

....

....

What was good?

....

....

What could be better?

....

....

What will you do to improve?

....

....

....

Easy Peasy
Pearl of Wisdom:
ENRICHMENT

If you're like me, then your dog definitely enriches your life, so it's only fair we return the compliment as much as we can. Every man and his dog knows that dogs need plenty of physical exercise, but what about their mental exercise needs?

Our dogs are superheroes with phenomenal senses and ninja-like physical prowess. They have hundreds of years of selective breeding to perform many jobs including tracking, hunting, searching and chasing. Too often, they're resigned to the role of professional couch potato, overfed yet undernourished. Let's be honest, if we don't give them a job, they'll go self-employed, and we'll have no one to blame but ourselves.

Adding extra enrichment into your dog's life can be a low financial, time and effort cost to you, but will deliver a huge beneficial dividend to your dog's daily routine.

Enrichment activities should tick at least one of the boxes below and, if you're smart, satisfy more than one!

Sensory

Does the activity stimulate and use any of your dog's senses: touch, sight, sound, taste and, of course, the biggy for all dogs, smell?

Feeding

Does the activity offer a novel, interesting or challenging way for your dog to earn their food? Remember, dogs are natural scavengers, hunters and rippers! How can you tap into that?

Social

Let's be honest, we all live busy lives and often wish there were more hours in the day. Sometimes enrichment activities can be a great way to entertain your dog if you're consumed elsewhere in a non-canine role. However, don't underestimate the power of you being involved in your dog's enrichment activities. Think of the bond, fun and relationships people build exercising with others in football or hockey teams, as opposed to solitary gym sessions. Dogs love enrichment activities, and they'll love you even more if you're part of the picture!

Below are a few suggestions to get you going on the enrichment front, but don't be shy, try a few of your own ideas, be creative. No one's watching and your dog won't judge you!

Rules

- Be Safe. Avoid choke hazards or unsafe materials.
- Set a difficulty level that encourages problem-

solving confidence and rewards effort.

🐾 Don't set tasks so hard they promote frustration. Think 'end of school term fun activities', not 'first day of summer exams'!

Enrichment Suggestions

Muff'in Tumble!

Place a tennis ball in each of the dozen or so moulds of a muffin tin. Under 5 of the balls, hide a treat. Encourage your dog to use their nose to sniff out the treats, their paw to move the balls and their mouth to enjoy the sweet taste of victory!

(Got a diddy little dog? No problem, go for treats hidden under screwed-up balls of paper neatly positioned in an egg box)

Interactive Feeders

Rather than feeding your dog from a boring old bowl, consider how you can extend the joy of mealtimes, add a bit more activity and increase the duration of, let's be honest, for most dogs, the highlight of each day!

🐾 Stuff your dog's meal into one, or several, Kong toys so they can receive not only the food, but also the feel-good chemicals their brain releases when they're simply kickin' back and chewing.

- In the summertime, freeze the stuffed Kong to create an enrichment ice lolly.

- Pop a few treats into a toilet or kitchen roll tube, fold over the ends and let your dog show off their killer prowess!

- Roll up a towel, tactically placing a few treats every few inches for your dog to discover as they roll/shake/'kill' the towel.

- Place some treats into an empty plastic bottle. Make sure you remove the cap and ring around the bottle neck first and, if your dog's a tough chewer, supervise to ensure safety. The rattling noise will definitely not get on your nerves!

Rip-Roaring Fun

Stuff an old split football or rugby ball with lots of rags. Leave a few pieces of rags poking out of the holes in the ball and encourage your dog to start pulling the rags out. Dogs are programmed to enjoy the 'dissecting prey' element of their feeding routines. This game is far more palatable than the real thing!

Treasure Hunt

Dogs love to follow their nose to find their 'treasure'. Be as creative as you fancy. You can head on out into the garden to lay a Hansel & Gretel-style trail of treats for your dog to follow and enjoy, or even head out with a handful of stuffed Kongs and tactically hide them in several places around the garden. Bonus points if, once the treasure is hidden, you go out *with* your dog and the pair of you go *hunting* together. Your dog will love the pair of you searching together as a team. For me, one of the joys of getting old is that once I've hidden them, I've already forgotten where they are, so the pair of us genuinely have to get our search on!

Alternatively, you can take the lazy option: open the back door, throw a handful of treats onto the lawn like you're feeding chickens and say to your dog, 'Go on, mate, off you go!' It'll cost you 10 seconds to set up, and create 30 minutes of joy for your dog. What a deal!

Dog
TRAINING

★ IS A ★
PROCESS
★ NOT AN ★
EVENT

WEEK 13

Rock Around

The Clock #1

Challenge: Rock Around The Clock #1

The final exercise we're going to master – and it's a biggie – is the showstopper known as Around the Clock!

What if I was to make a bet with you now, that by the end of your Around the Clock training, you'll be able to Recall your dog to run *past* a slice of ham on the floor to get to you! Fancy that bet?

It's not going to be straightforward, but together we can do it, Easy Peasy.

You're going to pull together several elements I've already introduced you to earlier, so make sure you're up to speed with your:

🐾 Supersonic Sits

🐾 Look To Say Please

🐾 Total Recalls

🐾 Hand Touch

🐾 And all the above with super-high Distraction!

The Target: The Clock Foundations

Go steady here. You and your dog are going to be working with a lot of different training elements PLUS plenty of added Distraction and Duration. Even at this base level, Around the Clock is a real test of self-control for all concerned!

Our first brief is to weave together our strong core exercises of Supersonic Sits and Look To Say Please, smother them with plenty of Distraction and Duration and allow them to become a rock-solid foundation on which our Around the Clock showstopper will be built.

To limit reinforced errors, I strongly recommend you start this exercise with a long line loosely attached to your dog's harness!

The Training

1. Grab yourself a bowl. Now, imagine there is a drawing of a huge clock face on the floor. Place the upturned bowl in the centre of the clock face. Stand next to your dog, 2 steps from the bowl, halfway between the bowl and 6 on the clock face.

2. With your dog remaining in a Sit, *slowly* place a treat on top of the bowl and return to stand next to your dog's side. Only when your dog glances up to your eyes, say, 'Good!' (to mark the behaviour) and bend down to point out the treat they can have (if they haven't beaten you to it already!). Keep practising until you can achieve 5 consecutive successful repetitions.

3. Ask your dog to Sit, load up the bowl with the treat and rather than returning to stand *next* to your dog, I want you to stand a pace directly behind them. (Be careful not to tread on their tail!) When they're **amazing** enough to look *away* from the treat and glance over their shoulder to you, say, 'Good!' and release them to the food.

Tip: If your dog keeps getting out of their Sit when you
try to load the bowl, break the process down so it's:

1. 'Sit', half step towards bowl, return and reinforce.

2. 'Sit', 1 step towards bowl, return and reinforce.

3. 'Sit', 2 steps towards bowl and half a bend,
   return and reinforce.

4. . . . and so on . . .

Easy Peasy Ponder Points

🐾 How reliable is your dog's Sit when you move *slowly* to place the treat on the bowl? (Slow movements from you means less Distraction, but more Duration.)

....

....

....

🐾 How reliable is your dog's Sit when you move at a faster pace to place the treat on the bowl? (Fast movements from you means less Duration, but more Distraction.)

....

....

....

🐾 On a scale of 1 to 10, how confident are you that you'll ever be able to get your dog to Recall OVER a slice of ham to get to you?

....

....

....

What was good?

....

....

....

....

What could be better?

....

....

....

....

What will you do to improve?

....

....

....

....

Doggy Diary

Write down all the amazing things you did with your dog this week!

Monday and Tuesday

....

....

....

Wednesday and Thursday

....

....

....

Friday

....

....

....

Saturday and Sunday

....

....

....

WEEK 14

Boomerangs

#2

Challenge: Boomerangs #2

The Target: Adding distance, adding objects

I'm guessing that if you're the adventurous sort (you know the type, someone who gets a cheeky henna tattoo on their holibobs or partakes in a 'you only live once' coffee after midday kinda rascal), at this point not only can you now get a reliable Boomerang from one metre, but you've also experimented by sending your dog around a few different objects. Let's start to add some more distance and throw a few more real-life objects into the equation . . .

The Training

1. From 1 metre, send your dog clockwise around the object. Remember to say, 'Good' as their right shoulder brushes the back of the object, then reinforce as they return to you.

2. After each successful repetition, take a further step backwards to increase the distance of your next Boomerang. If unsuccessful, go back to 1 metre and build up again, one step at a time. Set a target of 10 steps before you go to bed!

3. Go back to 1 metre, but now start Boomeranging your dog around objects you find on your daily walks: goal posts, park bins, trees, other people with their permission/forgiveness (delete as appropriate!).

Easy Peasy Ponder Points

🐾 As a bonus track, start saying, 'COME!' once they've circled the object and rush back towards you. After a few days, what have you noticed about your day-to-day Recalls?

....

....

....

🐾 List 5 new objects you can use for your Boomerangs on your daily walk. List in order of novelty:

1. ....

2. ....

3. ....

4. ....

5. ....

🐾 Next session, do 10 repetitions. What's your target distance? 5m? 10m? 15m?

....

....

....

What was good?

....

....

....

....

What could be better?

....

....

....

....

What will you do to improve?

....

....

....

....

Doggy Diary

Write down all the amazing things you did with your dog this week!

Monday and Tuesday

....
....
....

Wednesday and Thursday

....
....
....

Friday

....
....
....

Saturday and Sunday

....
....
....

WEEK 15

Peek-A-Boo

#2

Challenge: Peek-A-Boo #2

The Target: Adding the cue and building Duration

Now that you've both learned the Peek-A-Boo position, you need to add a verbal cue so that in the future you can ask for the behaviour. Also, by building Duration, you will help your dog learn that sometimes you will want them to hold the position for longer, perhaps in a vet's waiting room where space might be tight and safety is paramount.

The Training

1. As your dog returns to between your legs, count a second, feed them in position, count 2 seconds, feed in position, count 5 seconds, feed in position and then throw a treat out in front for your dog to go get, so you can turn your back and re-set for the next repetition.

2. Just as your dog sneaks their head between your legs to assume their position, say the cue, 'PEEK-A-BOO', when they're in the correct location, feed, count 3 seconds, feed again, count 6 seconds, feed, then throw a treat out in front so you can re-set.

3. As soon as your dog picks up the thrown treat, turn your back, open your legs and say, 'PEEK-A-BOO' to give a clear label and instruction to the behaviour that's going to follow, namely your dog putting their head between your legs. When in situ, count to 5 seconds, say, 'Good' and treat.

4. Re-set and repeat.

Easy Peasy Ponder Points

🐾 Is the time between each feeding sufficient to maintain interest, but also to build duration?

....

....

🐾 Are you giving the cue 'Peek-A-Boo' with a consistent tone and volume, to allow your dog to learn what the cue means?

....

....

🐾 Can you build a longer duration between treats?

....

....

🐾 Is your dog's head central and looking up to you when feeding?

....

....

What was good?

....

....

....

....

What could be better?

....

....

....

....

What will you do to improve?

....

....

....

....

Doggy Diary

Write down all the amazing things you did with your dog this week!

Monday and Tuesday

....

....

....

Wednesday and Thursday

....

....

....

Friday

....

....

....

Saturday and Sunday

....

....

....

WEEK 16

Look To Say Please #2

Challenge: Look To Say Please #2

The Target: Changing the picture

Now that you're getting regular Eye Contact with you seated, it's time to change the picture. I want your dog to look at you, regardless of what position or location you're in.

The Training

1. Stay seated. However, this time, if the treats were previously in your right hand, change them over so they're trapped in your left fist, and your left arm is extended. Let your dog investigate and when they look to you, say, 'Good', bring your two hands together in front of you, and treat your dog.

2. Next up, have the treats in your right fist, but this time <u>stand up</u>. When they look to you, say, 'Good', bring your two hands together in front of you, and treat your dog.

3. Stay <u>standing</u>, but mix it up again by having the treats in your left fist...

4. Once you're getting several quick successes with the set-ups above, start to shake your hand a little like you're waving a flag – the added movement of your fist will be more of a visual challenge for your dog to look away from, and will therefore act as a great exercise to consolidate all that you've both learned so far.

Easy Peasy Ponder Points

🐾 Which position were you in that took longest for
your dog to give you Eye Contact?

....

....

🐾 Where can you practise to add a little extra
Distraction, but maintain the target behaviour?

....

....

🐾 How long does it take for the pair of you to score
10 out of 10?

....

....

🐾 Is the timing of your 'Good' better at the beginning
or the end of each session?

....

....

What was good?

....

....

....

....

What could be better?

....

....

....

....

What will you do to improve?

....

....

....

....

Easy Peasy
Pearl of Wisdom:
BODY LANGUAGE

To be the very best owner, trainer and friend to your dog that you can be, I want to help you become a canine body-expert.

The greatest skill that any dog owner can possess is to be able to read – and **act upon** – what our dogs are telling us. Believe it or not, dogs are always telling us about how they're feeling. If they're happy, upset, stressed or jubilant, you can be sure they're communicating that flood of emotions through their body language, in the hope that someone's listening.

As a friend and supporter of your dog, it's important to accept that true communication doesn't start when your dog *talks* to you, it starts when you *listen*, and *respond*. If your dog has faith that you're the kind of friend who will listen and help them out when they need it, then they'll feel less inclined to shout or take matters into their own hands when they feel under pressure. On the flip side, they'll also flourish in the knowledge that you're there to rejoice and celebrate the good times with them. Like when they find a dead pigeon or fox poo to roll in!

I bet you and I have our own little quirks we do when we're happy or stressed. Of course, we do, we're individuals, and so is your dog! Spend some time over the next few days observing your dog when they're relaxed, in a neutral environment with not much going on. Once you're familiar with their body language *benchmarks*, you'll then find it much easier to recognise when their body language changes to illustrate elements of, for example, joy or concern.

No one part of a dog's body will tell you the whole picture, but what you can do is observe and read all the individual elements: tail, eyes, mouth and so on, to then make an educated guess as to whether your dog needs your support.

Warning: context is everything. Never look at your dog's body language in isolation; always look at the environment they're in and consider what else might be going on.

For example, your dog is panting. Perhaps they're stressed. Or . . . perhaps it's warm and your dog's been wrestling a teddy bear for the last 20 minutes!

Let's imagine your dog's pupils are dilated. Perhaps they're aroused because they can smell the neighbourhood cat.

Body Language Benchmarks

Over the next couple of days, I'd love for you to observe your dog when they're nice and relaxed and fill in the table opposite to create your neutral Body Language Benchmarks:

BODY PART	WHEN NEUTRAL
Eyes	
Ears	
Mouth	
Spine	
Tail	
Hips	
Coat	
Feet	

Here's a few tips to look out for regarding body language that may suggest an opportunity to support your dog:

BODY PART	OBSERVATIONS	CONSIDERATIONS
Eyes ☺	*A happy, relaxed dog generally has a soft brow and diverts their gaze regularly*	
Eyes ☹	Hard. Staring. More white of the eye showing than usual. Dilated pupils.	Is your dog comfortable? Are they feeling threatened? Are they worried about losing a resource? Over-aroused? Can you help ease the pressure for them?
Ears ☺	*A happy relaxed dog has soft, mobile ears with no tension*	

Ears ☹	Is the base of the ear lower than normal? Pinned back? Erect?	Is there a threatening noise such as thunder or fireworks? Can you distance your dog from something they may be afraid of?
Mouth ☺	*You can often see the bottom teeth of a dog who's happy as the muscles in the jaw are nice and relaxed.*	
Mouth ☹	Tight. Closed. Pulled forward. Rapid tongue flicks.	What's happening that may be making your dog stressed or over-aroused? How can you help?
Spine ☺	*A relaxed dog will have a soft, flexible spine that comfortably 'flows' as they move.*	
Spine ☹	Stiff. Hard. Straight, flat line from nose to tail. Cowering.	Is your dog too intensely focused on a perceived threat, or about to chase with bad intentions!?
Tail ☺	*A happy 'greeting' tail will 'helicopter' in circles or make erratic figure of 8 movements! When your dog is nicely relaxed and joyful, the tail's motions will influence a soft movement of their hips.*	

Tail ☹	May be tucked between your dog's back legs or held high arching over their back. Does the tail move but the hips stay stiff and hard?	Is your dog feeling threatened, or threatening?
Coat ☺	*A content dog will have a relaxed coat, a healthy sheen and the hair will lay comfortably (breed permitting!)*	
Coat ☹	Is your dog's coat dry, shedding excessive dandruff and hair? Is the hair between the shoulders erect? Are there bald patches or areas when the coat doesn't sit comfortably?	Is your dog experiencing excessive or unnecessary stress? How can you relieve them of that concern?
Feet ☺	*Relaxed toes and feet that are soft to flex with movement.*	
Feet ☹	Are the toes unusually scrunched, like a fist?	Your dog may be feeling tense. What can you change in their environment to help?

If there's ONE thing your dog wants you to do, it's for you to understand them. How amazing it is to have a friend that knows how you're feeling, and knows how to make you feel better?

Never stop observing, analysing and acting on what you see. On behalf of all dogs you'll ever meet, thank you, it really helps!

🐾 When does your dog ever look unhappy and how can you tell?

....

🐾 What can you do to reduce or eliminate that unhappiness?

....

🐾 When does your dog look their happiest and how can you tell?

....

🐾 What unusual way does your dog show you they're happy? (My little Chihuahua Nancy pumps her front feet up and down like she's in *Riverdance*, whereas my Staffie Pablo snorts!)

....

🐾 What do *you* do with *your* body that lets your dog know you're happy? (Whatever it is, do more of it, it's good for you!)

....

WEEK 17

Supersonic Sits

#2

Challenge: Supersonic Sits #2

The Target: Shifting the perspective

In real life, no matter where you're stood in relation to your dog's location, it's great to know that Sit means Sit. We do this by proofing the behaviour. Following Challenge #1's Ponder Points, we've already started to *proof* the Sit behaviour by practising in a variety of locations. Now I want you to go a step further by achieving the same great results even when the training environment is different.

The Training

1. With your dog standing in front of you, use your verbal cue to ask your dog to Sit. When they do, reinforce and repeat 5 times.

2. With your dog on your *left-hand* side, use your verbal cue to ask them to Sit. If they need a little more help, use your hand signal to lure the behaviour. Following each success, fade your hand signal a little more each time until it's no longer required.

3. Repeat Point 2 for your other hand.

4. Practise the above 3 stages first with your dog off-lead, then with the lead attached. Practise inside and outside in a variety of locations. Keep your cues, your timing and your generosity the same. It's only the environment that needs to change!

5. If you are happy that all of the above are rock solid it's time to raise the stakes! I want you to be able to turn your back on your dog to then ask for a Sit. This is a real rock 'n' roll level of shifting the perspective,

so if successful, you both deserve a treat! If your dog keeps swinging around to face you, either get a friend to hold your dog's lead or put them behind a child-gate or fence (the dog, not the friend!) – you may need a cunning system of mirrors set up so that you can see the results!

Easy Peasy Ponder Points

Does it feel like your dog has a bias to want to be on a particular side? Which side is that?

....

....

Is the timing of your 'Good' still on point? How can you improve it?

....

....

Other than turning your back, can you think of any other ways to change your dog's perspective, but rise to the challenge of 'Sit means Sit'?

....

....

Can you practise on a variety of surfaces?

....

....

Have you managed to practise in a variety of weather conditions?

....

....

Can you practise on a variety of surfaces?

....

....

What was good?

....

....

What could be better?

....

....

What will you do to improve?

....

....

Doggy Diary

Write down all the amazing things you did with your dog this week!

Monday and Tuesday

....

....

....

Wednesday and Thursday

....

....

....

Friday

....

....

....

Saturday and Sunday

....

....

....

WEEK 18
The Magic Hand
Touch #2

Challenge: The Magic Hand Touch #2

The Target: When you love it, name it!

Now that you're getting a nice, fluent Nose-To-Hand touch each time you flourish your left or right hand, it's time to name the behaviour by giving it a verbal cue. By having a verbal cue, you can then start to ask for the behaviour even if your dog's not looking at you.

The Training

1. With your dog facing you, present your target hand from behind your back and say, 'Touch'. As soon as their nose makes contact, say, 'Good', remove your hand and give your dog a treat from the other hand.

2. Swap hands. A split-second before the nose makes contact, say the cue, 'Touch', then when contact is made say, 'Good' and reinforce.

3. When your dog's not looking at you, produce your hand with a flourish as you say, 'Touch' to *cue* the behaviour. As soon as they do, *mark* the behaviour with a 'Good' and reinforce.

4. Offer your hand in different positions: between your legs, up high, down low. The only thing holding you back now is your own imagination (and flexibility!)

Easy Peasy Ponder Points

🐾 Name 5 areas you can practise your skills together to really make the Hand Touch reliable.

1. ....

2. ....

3. ....

4. ....

5. ....

🐾 Other than treats, what else does your dog love that you could use to reinforce the Hand Touch?

....

....

....

🐾 What differences have you observed between practising inside or outdoors?

....

....

....

What was good?

....

....

....

....

What could be better?

....

....

....

....

What will you do to improve?

....

....

....

....

Doggy Diary

Write down all the amazing things you did with your dog this week!

Monday and Tuesday

....

....

....

Wednesday and Thursday

....

....

....

Friday

....

....

....

Saturday and Sunday

....

....

....

WEEK 19

The Smiling Lead

#2

Challenge: The Smiling Lead #2

The Target: Adding movement

Now that you're getting regular Eye Contact from your dog when they're on-lead stationary next to you, it's time to add a bit of movement so we can start heading in the direction of the final picture we want for The Smiling Lead.

By you walking as you hold your dog's lead, be aware that we're really raising the bar, as not only are we adding movement for you, but also movement for your dog AND we're adding new Distractions as the pair of you walk over different smells on the ground (you may not smell them, but a pound to a penny your dog does!).

The Training

1. With your dog in their harness and you holding the lead, slowly start moving with tiny steps to the side. With your dog following you, say, 'Good!' and drop a treat every time they look up to you.

2. Keep moving with slow, small steps: sometimes to the left, then to the right. Walk backwards and in small semicircles . . . as you move, the second your dog looks up to you, say, 'Good!' and drop the treat for them.

3. Now the checking-in on the move is nice and smooth, rather than dropping the treat for your dog when they look up to you on the move, I want you to place the treat directly into their mouth. We're now reinforcing not only the checking-in on the move, but we're also showing your dog where the best place to hang out is when they're on-lead with you: that's right, next to your leg. Happy days!

Easy Peasy Ponder Points

🐾 Movement – could your movement be smoother? Avoid straight lines as that may encourage your dog to forge ahead. Stay smooth, stay slow and change direction every 5 steps or so. Write down how you might do that.

....

....

🐾 Timing – reinforce the Eye Contact on the move by saying, 'Good!' the moment your dog glances to you. When has this worked? When hasn't this worked? Why?

....

....

🐾 Payment – physically looking up to you on the movement may be tricky for your dog, so make sure you pay well for effort! When has this worked? When hasn't this worked? Why?

....

....

What was good?

....

....

....

....

What could be better?

....

....

....

....

What will you do to improve?

....

....

....

....

Doggy Diary

Write down all the amazing things you did
with your dog this week!

Monday and Tuesday

....

....

....

Wednesday and Thursday

....

....

....

Friday

....

....

....

Saturday and Sunday

....

....

....

WEEK 20

The Seek Back

#2

Challenge: The Seek Back #2

The Target: Using the Seek Back as a reward

By now you should have completed 100s (YES, HUNDREDS!) of Seek Backs with your dog. If you have (no fibbing!), then as soon as they hear you say, 'Find It!', I'm hoping that a flame of excitement is ignited in their belly as they turn their sniffing powers up to 10 to search and find their treasure.

Yes? Good!

Now that your dog loves to hear the phrase 'Find It', we can use a Seek Back to reinforce the behaviours *you* want to see.

NB: From this point, the dropped item can be a treat pouch, a toy, a Tupperware box of ham . . . whatever your dog adores.

The Training

1. Walk with your dog on lead then subtly drop the item as you continue to forge ahead . . .

2. You're ready to perform your Seek Back cue, but <u>only</u> when your dog glances up to you on the move. The second your eyes meet then BOOM, say, 'Find It!', guide them around 180 degrees and the pair of you get your search on.

3. We're in a win–win situation here. You're using the Seek Back to reinforce Eye Contact on the move, which in turn means more Smiling Lead. Perfect!

Easy Peasy Ponder Points

🐾 What other individual behaviours can you reinforce with a Seek Back in your next session?

....

....

....

🐾 Where can you practise your Seek Backs off-lead this week?

....

....

....

🐾 What has been your dog's favourite item to find so far?

....

....

....

What was good?

....

....

....

....

What could be better?

....

....

....

....

What will you do to improve?

....

....

....

....

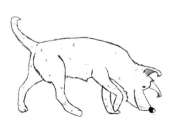

Easy Peasy
Pearl of Wisdom:
GROOMING

Dogs, like us chimps, are social animals. Individuals in a social group rely on each other, so it's important to make sure we're each in tip-top condition. The ritual of grooming feels so good to us social mammals that we're prepared to pay top dollar for a visit to the spa. Even when times are hard, there's no greater pleasure than pulling a few nits out of your mate's hair while you're watching the football . . . no? Just me, then!

The benefits of grooming your dog are many:

Social bonding

Nothing warms my heart more than when I'm grooming my own dog, they then turn around and start nibbling and grooming me back with their front teeth to return the compliment. Be still my beating heart!

Visual inspection

As you're handling your dog, take the opportunity to make sure all areas look healthy: eyes, ears, nose and mouth. Check the coat for any unwanted parasite lodgers and look between the toes to make sure no nasties such as splinters or grass seed have sneaked in there to cause discomfort.

Tactile inspection

I always start my grooming sessions with a nice massage. Not only does the massage relax my dog, but it also gives me a chance to release any dead hair, loosen any dry dirt and to feel for any lumps and bumps, cuts or grazes before I go in with my brushes. By massaging my dogs daily, I know I'm as familiar as possible with their bodies, so if a lump *does* appear, I know I'm going to detect it sooner rather than later.

Skin maintenance

By giving your dog a nice, thorough daily massage, not only are you loosening up the dead hair and dirt prior to brushing, but you're also activating the sebaceous glands on your dog's skin. When massaged, the sebaceous glands secrete sebum, which is the natural oil that keeps your dog's skin and hair supple, shiny and ready for anything! Sebum™ 'You know they're worth it.'

The sniff test!

This may sound odd, but I'm in the habit of sniffing my dog's ears and breath each time I groom them. I'm not sniffing to find out if they smell – of course they do, they're only human – but I want to discover if the smell has *changed*. A change in the smell of a dog's breath may suggest potential tooth decay or a digestion issue, whereas an odd smell from a dog's ear may warrant further investigation to ensure no food or sneaky creepy crawlies have lodged in there, rent free!

Grooming your dog is an important habit to create, but also has the potential to be a pleasurable experience for the both of you.

Here are a few suggestions to help you brush up on your skills, comb over the suggestions and see what information you can tease out. (I know.)

- Always brush in the direction of the hair growth.
- Don't try to do too much too soon. If your dog is new to grooming and a little wary, do short, gentle sessions and ensure the experience is pleasurable for your dog by following each gentle stroke of the brush with a tiny treat.

Different tools suit different types of coat:
- Rakes are great for long coats and dogs with a thick undercoat.
- Rubber brushes suit shorter coats and do a fab job of removing dead hair and massaging the skin.
- Bristle brushes are the way to go to finish off a grooming session or when you want to give your dog a quick 'once-over' before visitors arrive!
- Short-coated dogs really benefit from the use

of a grooming mitt, which has short rubber bobbles on the palms to slick back the hair.

Bathing Tips:

- 🐾 Don't wash too often. We don't want to constantly strip the coat of its own natural and protective oils.
- 🐾 Remove all knots and tangles *before* you wet your dog.
- 🐾 Soak the coat thoroughly prior to shampooing.
- 🐾 For longer-coated dogs, dilute the shampoo in water first to make the application easier.
- 🐾 To ensure correct PH levels, use a purpose-made dog shampoo.
- 🐾 Don't shampoo your dog's face, ears or mouth. Instead wipe with a clean wet cloth.
- 🐾 Rinse thoroughly to avoid irritation.
- 🐾 Brace yourself for the SHAKE-OFF!
- 🐾 Towel dry as much as possible.
- 🐾 If using a hair dryer, slowly introduce your dog to the sight and sound of the dryer over many sessions *prior* to having to use it for real. Never have the dryer too hot!

Remember, your most important grooming tools are your eyes and your hands. Look at grooming sessions as an extra opportunity to build and confirm your relationship with your dog.

WEEK 21
Total Recalls
#2

Challenge: Total Recalls #2

The Target: Circuit Recalls

Now we've paired the phrase 'COME!' with the good times with you, you'll be getting Reflex-like focus from your dog as soon as you use that magic word. Now that your dog knows what 'COME!' means when they hear it, it's time to add the behaviour of them running to you in anticipation of the pay-out!

It's time to introduce Circuit Recalls!

The Training

1. Head outside to a safe space with your dog. If needs be, feel free to have a long line of 5 metres or so trailing on the ground behind your dog so they can't run off and get the pair of you into trouble

2. Next, imagine a triangle on the ground, with each point of the triangle 5 metres away from each of the other two points.

3. Stand at triangle point A with your dog, shout 'COME!', place 3 treats by your feet for your dog to enjoy as you run away to point B of the triangle.

4. With you arrived at point B, wait until your dog finishes their treats and their head comes up off the floor, then shout 'COME!', again place 3 treats by your feet, and as your dog runs to point B, you take off with the speed of a puma to point C.

5. As soon as your dog finishes their treats at point B and lifts their head, shout 'COME!' with the joy of Charlie finding Wonka's golden ticket and drop 3 more treats by your feet before heading back over to point A . . .

6. Keep going around your triangle, shouting 'COME!' and placing treats by your feet for your dog to run to and enjoy before dashing to the next point. When you're spent, crash on the floor and, as your dog runs to you, have a good play and cuddle for as long as it takes for you to get your breath back!

7. Over several sessions, increase the distance between the three points of the triangle.

8. To test your speed, go from 3 treats, to 2, to 1! Less treats means you'll have to shift faster to be in position and ready to shout 'COME!' as soon as your dog raises their head from the previous point of the triangle! Who knows, maybe we've another Olympic sprinter in the making?!

Easy Peasy Ponder Points

🐾 Timing: are you calling your dog _only_ when they raise their head after enjoying the treats? Any sooner and you'll be teaching them to ignore you, as they'll be hearing your call but having a great time _away_ from you!

....

🐾 Could you use even better treats to turbo boost the Recall? How about warm sausages?!

....

🐾 Are you consistent with the way that you call your dog? Rehearse what you'll ultimately want to see at the park – a consistent word, tone and volume now will pay dividends in the future.

....

What was good?

....

What could be better?

....

What will you do to improve?

....

Doggy Diary

Write down all the amazing things you did with your dog this week!

Monday and Tuesday

....

....

....

Wednesday and Thursday

....

....

....

Friday

....

....

....

Saturday and Sunday

....

....

....

WEEK 22
Detection Dog
#2

Challenge: Detection Dog #2

The Target: Searching the room

With your dog successfully targeting and indicating the loaded pot with their nose, it's time to move the search area away from your hands, and into a larger area. By introducing a room search, you're planting the seed that when you say 'Find It', the target could be anywhere in the environment. This will help you increase your search areas in the future, so your detection work will not only be mentally rewarding, but it can also become a good physical exercise for your dog!

For this stage, I want you to grab three saucepans from your kitchen . . .

The Training

1. Let your dog see you place the treat-loaded pot under one saucepan on the floor. Ask your dog to 'Find It!' and when they sniff under the pan, say, 'Good', lift the pan, unscrew the pot lid and give your dog plenty of treats.

2. Repeat Step 1, but this time when you say, 'Good', give your dog a treat from your pocket, so you don't have to keep loading the pot.

3. Introduce pans two and three onto the floor. Randomly mix up the pan layout so your dog has to search all three to find the target treat pot. When they do, say, 'Good' and make a huge fuss of your dog.

4. Evolve your sessions to add some duration of their Indication behaviour. Remember, the Indication is when the dog locates the scent with their nose and tells you they have found the treasure. The longer the length of the Indication, the better the chance you have of spotting it! Sometimes wait 1 second before saying, 'Good', sometimes, 3 seconds, sometimes 5 . . .

5. Mix up the layout on the floor, add a few more pans, perhaps your colander and fruit bowl. In fact, throw the kitchen sink at it!

Easy Peasy Ponder Points

🐾 Would a heavier pan allow the dog to add duration to their Indication, as opposed to pushing the pan out of the way?

....

🐾 Could you improve your 'sleight of hand' when hiding the pot?

....

🐾 How can you make sure your dog is sniffing and facing the target when you say, 'Good'?

....

🐾 Could you be more creative with your hides? Different objects, levels, rooms?

....

🐾 Are you both enjoying the process?

....

🐾 How could you make it more enjoyable?

....

What was good?

....
....
....
....

What could be better?

....
....
....
....

What will you do to improve?

....
....
....
....

Doggy Diary

Write down all the amazing things you did with your dog this week!

Monday and Tuesday

....

....

....

Wednesday and Thursday

....

....

....

Friday

....

....

....

Saturday and Sunday

....

....

....

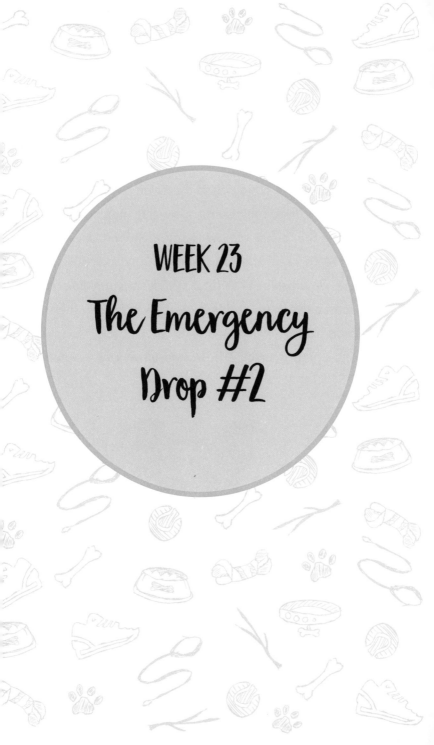

WEEK 23

The Emergency Drop #2

Challenge: The Emergency Drop #2

The Target: Introduce the items

Now that you've conditioned the value of your Drop cue, it's time to introduce some low-value items so we can maintain the behaviour we want, build on success and continue to layer the foundations for a rock-solid Drop in any circumstances. We don't need your dog to be picking up the items at this stage, they're merely there as a building block.

Right, grab yourself a book and an empty Tupperware box . . .

The Training

1. Quietly place the book on the floor, let your dog check it out and after a couple of seconds say, 'Drop' . . . as they run to you, place one treat by your feet for them to scoff, then toss the second treat away from you for your dog to chase.

2. This time, slide the book along the floor. As your dog glances towards its movement, say, 'Drop', and reinforce twice as before. The additional movement of the item is tougher for your dog to resist.

3. Quietly place your Tupperware box on the floor, then same procedure – let your dog check it out and after a couple of seconds say, 'Drop'. Again, as they run to you, place one treat by your feet, and toss the second treat from them to enjoy.

4. Slide the Tupperware box along the floor, and as your dog glances towards its movement, say, 'Drop', and reinforce twice as before.

Easy Peasy Ponder Points

🐾 List 5 other safe options you could use as items:

1. ....
2. ....
3. ....
4. ....
5. ....

🐾 Is there a time of day your dog seems more responsive?

....

....

....

🐾 Can you see evidence of your dog waiting for the second treat? If so, good news! That'll stop them grabbing treat 1 then rushing back to the 'dangerous' item.

....

....

....

What was good?

....
....
....
....

What could be better?

....
....
....
....

What will you do to improve?

....
....
....
....

Doggy Diary

Write down all the amazing things you did with your dog this week!

Monday and Tuesday

....

....

....

Wednesday and Thursday

....

....

....

Friday

....

....

....

Saturday and Sunday

....

....

....

WEEK 24
Hit The Brakes
#2

Challenge: Hit The Brakes #2

The Target: Getting the Behaviour

Now that you've spent plenty of time getting your dog to know what, 'Stop!' means to *them*, it's time to check that you're getting the behaviour *you* want when you give the **cue**. To check that everything's on track, you're going to cue the behaviour, **get** the behaviour, then **reinforce** the behaviour. Sounds simple on paper, doesn't it!? Don't worry, we can do this, the pressure's on me . . .

The Training

1. To remind your dog what this game is all about, drop 5 treats on the floor and as they munch on those, sneak your 5 or so metres away and get ready.

2. As soon as they finish their treats and the head comes up, say, 'Stop!', give the correct body language signal, and toss a treat behind their butt to remind them what happens when the 'Stop!' cue is given. Repeat 2–3 times just to warm up for the next level.

3. Once your dog has eaten the previously thrown treat, they look up and start to wander towards you, say, 'Stop!', give the appropriate 'Traffic Police Officer' hand signal and wait. We're looking for your dog to halt; the second they do, say, 'GOOD!' and throw the treat behind their butt. BOOM! We're in business!

4. Now that your dog is stopping when you give the cue, don't be too greedy, but see if you can ask for a 'Stop', and count a couple of seconds of your dog stood still before you say, 'Good' and toss them the well-earned treat.

If your dog isn't actually stopping at this stage when you give the cue, no issue at all. It simply means you need to spend a little longer at stage 1 to 'charge-up' what the cue predicts. (Answer: a treat immediately landing behind their butt.)

Easy Peasy Ponder Points

🐾 Is your body language and silhouette as clear and consistent as possible? How could it be better?

....

....

🐾 How's your throwing? Could it be better?

....

....

🐾 Are you being too greedy with the duration between cue and throw?

....

....

🐾 Can you see evidence of 'learning' from your dog?

....

....

🐾 Is your verbal cue consistent?

....

....

What was good?

....

....

....

What could be better?

....

....

....

What will you do to improve?

....

....

....

Easy Peasy
Pearl of Wisdom:
K9 FIRST AID

You know me by now, I try to keep it light if I can, but (serious teacher's face) I don't want us to shy away from the importance of having a little K9 First Aid knowledge in our locker. It could be a matter of . . . well, you know the rest.

The main purpose of first aid is to prevent further injury and relieve pain until professional help can be administered.

Picture the scene: it's an emergency situation and your dog has been hurt, here's the plan:

- Ensure you and others are safe
- Keep calm. Assess, think and take first-aid action
- Be aware that your dog will be frightened and may try to bite out of fear
- Contact the vet
- Drive carefully

Pet first-aid kit

Put together a couple of K9 first-aid kits for yourself. I recommend a larger kit for your home and a smaller one to keep in the car. Remember, it may not just be your own dog that you're able to help one day, so account for breed sizes! Always have a couple of emergency vet telephone numbers in your phone and written on your K9 First-Aid Kit box.

Your first-aid kit should contain:

- A selection of bandages and dressings
- Foil blanket
- Blunt-ended scissors
- Sterile wound wash
- Cotton wool
- Tweezers
- Surgical tape
- Vinyl gloves
- Antiseptic wipes

Road Traffic Accident

Or as they say on the cool cop shows, **'R.T.A.!'**

If you are unlucky enough to be involved in a road traffic accident while your dog is with you, first of all, keep yourself safe. Make sure someone is there to stop oncoming traffic. If your dog is injured and immobile, lift, or roll them onto your coat and drag, to safety.

Check for any immediate life-threatening issues such as heavy bleeding or laboured breathing.

Keep the dog warm to resist going into shock.

Call and get to the vet urgently.

Sometimes you may come across a lone dog by the road that seems a bit lost and spaced-out. You may suspect that a vehicle has hit them. If they'll let you, a quick check to see if they have grazed pads may offer supporting evidence. If their pads are fine, perhaps they're just on their walk-of-shame from last night's rave.

BLEEDING
External Bleeding

If the bleeding is not too heavy, look to flush the wound out with clean tap or salted water to remove as much dirt as possible to prevent infection. If your dog is bleeding heavily, apply pressure to the wound with a clean dressing as a significant loss of blood could result in your dog collapsing, going into shock or worse. If no bones are broken, you can elevate the limb to allow gravity to help reduce the pressure in the injured area.

Internal Bleeding

To help an emergency vet prepare as quickly as possible, it's good to know that the signs of internal bleeding may be:

- A swollen stomach
- Pale gums
- Difficulty breathing
- Cold ears or feet

By observing and reporting on the above, you could give the vet – and therefore the dog – a potentially life-saving head-start.

Choking

Considering the amount of nonsense dogs put in their mouths, it's amazing that we're not all running around constantly removing items from in there like a substitute teacher on a nursery school outing to Willy Wonka's.

If your dog is choking, you need to act and you need to act **FAST**.

Hold the mouth open to try and see what and where the blockage is. If someone else is there to help, one of you can hold the mouth open while the other one looks for the blockage. If the dog is conscious, to avoid being bitten try to use a tool such as tweezers, a flat spoon handle or pliers to remove the object. If the dog is unconscious, guide your finger around the back of their throat to try and sweep the offending item out. If unsuccessful, either raise your dog's hind legs to try and tip the object out, thump between their shoulder blades, or lay your dog on their side, and with both hands, press firmly against their rib cage several times to muster the air in their lungs to force the object from its lodgings.

Insect Stings

If you've a dog that likes to hunt wasps, then stings are not uncommon. Not really a 'life-or-death' situation thankfully, unless your dog has a dreaded allergic reaction.

Signs of allergic reaction

- Collapse
- Breathing difficulty
- Cold ears or feet
- Swelling around the face
- Vomiting
- Diarrhoea

For even the slightest suspicion that your dog is having an allergic reaction to a sting, call your vet, explain the symptoms and, if advised, get them to the vet sharpish.

If there's no allergic reaction, you may be able to remove the sting yourself by pushing the dog's flesh below the point of the sting smoothly with a credit card. (If you're posh, use your gold card, if you're really posh, use your chauffeur's.)

To soothe the area, you can use bicarbonate of soda and water for bee stings, and vinegar for wasp stings.

I have a little mantra for remembering the difference: *'Bicarb For Bees; Vinegar For Vasps'*

Basic Health Signs

The best way to spot any sudden potential health concerns with your dog is to inspect and handle them regularly. That way, as soon as anything is out of the ordinary, it'll stand out like a sore dewclaw.

- Your dog should have 9 orifices: 2 eyes, 2 ears, 2 nostrils, 1 mouth, 1 anus, 1 penis or vulva (any more than 9, immediately call your local vet/newspaper/circus). Ensure that all orifices are clean. No discharge, redness, itchiness or nasty smell.

- Eyes should be bright and your dog should display no behaviour to suggest sensitivity to light.

- Gums should not be red, swollen or bleeding. A noticeable change in the smell of your dog's breath may suggest teeth or digestion issues.

- Regular massage will ensure (that your dog loves you, and . . .) you are alerted early to any lumps, bumps, cuts or grazes – also see grooming, page 170. Be aware of heavy dandruff that may suggest skin issues or excessive stress.

- Ensure your dog has no particular areas that are tender to the touch.

- Check the feet and toes are healthy. Red flags would be swelling, flaking, cracks, redness or excessive temperature.

Keep a close eye on your dog and never gamble with their health – you know they're just too precious.

WEEK 25
Say Your Prayers
#2

Challenge: Say Your Prayers #2

The Target: Two paws

You can now lure one paw onto the platform – now it's time to build on the confidence you've already created by luring the second paw.

The Training

1. Use a treat in your hand to encourage your dog to place their first front foot onto the platform. When the foot is in the correct position, treat, then immediately take a second treat and lure your dog a little further onto the platform so they put both feet onto the surface. When in place, feed several individual treats so your dog learns this is *the* place to be!

2. Next time, use the lure to encourage your dog to put both feet onto the platform and when in place, say, 'Good' (to mark the behaviour) and treat.

3. Next, rather than being on opposite sides, stand to the side of the platform and encourage your next 'paws-up' from there. As you lure your dog into position, say, 'Target' and as soon as their two front feet hit the platform say, 'Good' and treat them as they remain in position.

Easy Peasy Ponder Points

🐾 Are you able to expand the time between treats, to
increase the duration of the two-foot-position being
held?

....

....

....

🐾 What have you seen from your dog to suggest they're
beginning to learn what 'Target' means?

....

....

....

🐾 Try a couple of alternative platforms, one slightly
taller, one slightly shorter. List below in order of
comfort for your dog:

1. ....

2. ....

What was good?

....

....

....

....

What could be better?

....

....

....

....

What will you do to improve?

....

....

....

....

Doggy Diary

Write down all the amazing things you did with your dog this week!

Monday and Tuesday

....

....

....

Wednesday and Thursday

....

....

....

Friday

....

....

....

Saturday and Sunday

....

....

....

WEEK 26
Rock Around
The Clock #2

Challenge: Rock Around The Clock #2

The Target: Adding the Recall and Touch

Now that your dog is remaining in a Sit while you load up the bowl, and you're marking successful Eye Contact with a 'Good' prior to releasing them to the treat, it's time to bolt the Recall AND Hand Touch into the proceedings.

 212

The Training

1. With your dog now remaining in a Sit at '6' on the clock face, slowly place a treat on top of the bowl and return so you're standing 2 metres *behind* your dog. When your dog looks to you, with great animation say, 'COME!' and jog back a step or two. As soon as your dog gets to you say, 'Good!' and run with your dog towards the bowl so they can enjoy their prize!

Okay, okay, I know when it's written down it seems so easy! In real life? Maybe not so much. That's why God invented long lines to limit mistakes and why our Secret Top Tip of Humility is so important. If you hit a wall, don't be afraid to go back a step or two to an achievable level and build up again from there.

2. When you can reliably call your dog away from the bowl 5 times in a row, I want you to finally add a Hand Touch after the Recall before saying, 'Good!' and allowing your dog to dash back for their treat.

3. The successful picture at this stage should look like this:

a. Ask your dog to Sit at '6' on the clock face.

b. With your dog sitting, you head over and place a treat on top of the up turned bowl.

c. Return to stand 2 metres behind your dog.

d. When you dog **LOOKS** to you, say, **'COME!'**. When your dog gets to you say, **'TOUCH'**, your dog then touches their nose to your open palm before you say, **'GOOD!'** and release your dog to go get their well-earned treat.

Easy Peasy Ponder Points

Over the first 5 repetitions, how many times did you need to rely on your long line to prevent your dog from ignoring your Recall?

....

Over the second 5 repetitions, how many times did you need to rely on your long line to prevent your dog from ignoring your Recall?

....

🐾 List in order of fluency: Sit, Eye Contact, Recall, Touch:

....

🐾 On a scale of 1 to 10, how confident are you now that you'll ever be able to get your dog to Recall OVER a slice of ham to get to you?

....

....

What was good?

....

....

....

What could be better?

....

....

....

What will you do to improve?

....

....

....

Doggy Diary

Write down all the amazing things you did with your dog this week!

Monday and Tuesday

....

....

....

Wednesday and Thursday

....

....

....

Friday

....

....

....

Saturday and Sunday

....

....

....

WEEK 27

Boomerangs

#3

Challenge: Boomerangs #3

The Target: Double-Up

I reckon that by now you've done enough work with your Boomerang that you're fairly confident your dog will go around any appropriate object from a decent distance.

One object? Child's play.

Let's go Pro Level. It's time to Double-Up!

The Training

1. Grab two familiar objects you've Boomeranged around in the past. Place the objects 10 metres apart and then stand, with your dog, in the middle of them.

2. With your usual set-up, face Object 1, say, 'Boomer', give your hand signal and send your dog around; as soon as they circle Object 1 and start heading back towards you, turn your body through 180 degrees so you can then send them around Object 2 with your familiar hand signal and verbal cue of 'Boomer'. Once your dog has circled Object 2, say, 'Good' and reinforce like they've just scored the winner in the World Cup Final!

3. Run the double sequence a few times and when you're consistent, chance your arm with 3, 4, 5, maybe even 6 Boomerangs between the two objects per repetition. As you're now at expert level, there's no need to reinforce every turn; just throw a big party for your dog after the final lap!

Easy Peasy Ponder Points

🐾 Your cues now will need to start looking like a smooth, consistent dance; think Patrick Swayze on ice. List them here:

....

🐾 Practise first without your dog. What's the trickiest part?

....

🐾 How many times on your first session did you need to take a few steps to Object 2 in order to successfully Boomerang?

....

🐾 How many steps did you need to take on your fifth session?

....

🐾 What do you notice in your dog's performance when you swap your original Objects 1 and 2 for novel objects?

....

What do you notice from your dog's performance now that they don't get a treat for every single loop, only for a series of loops?

....

Why do you think there's a difference?

....

What was good?

....

....

....

What could be better?

....

....

....

What will you do to improve?

....

....

....

Doggy Diary

Write down all the amazing things you did with your dog this week!

Monday and Tuesday

....

....

....

Wednesday and Thursday

....

....

....

Friday

....

....

....

Saturday and Sunday

....

....

....

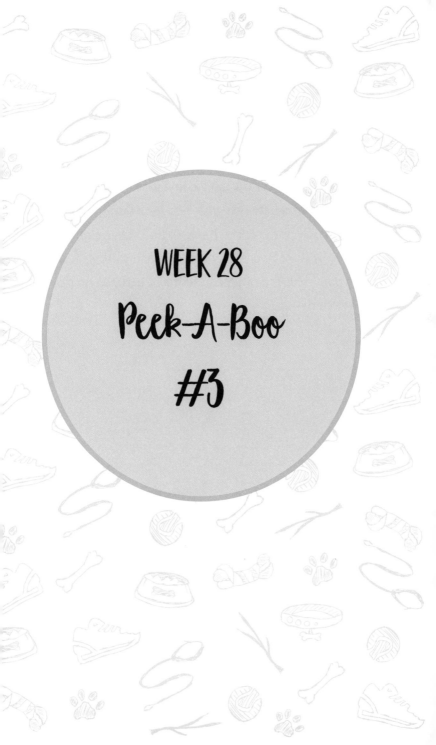

WEEK 28
Peek-A-Boo
#3

Challenge: Peek-A-Boo #3

The Target: Feet targeting

By this stage you should be able to say 'PEEK-A-BOO' for your dog to then comfortably come in from behind you and place their head between your legs for a duration of at least 5 seconds. (If not, back to Peek-A-Boo #2 you go!)

We now want your dog to place each of their front feet *onto yours*. This is a big ask in terms of trust, so go slowly to build confidence.

The Training

1. This time, before cueing 'PEEK-A-BOO', open your legs as before, but turn your toes inwards towards each other, like a massive bald duck.

2. Cue 'PEEK-A-BOO' as before, encourage your dog between your legs, but this time, lure their head into a position that allows one of their feet to land on your foot – then *as soon as* their *foot lands on yours*, gently feed several treats in position so your dog can get used to balancing on your foot. After a few seconds, toss a treat forward for your dog to go get, so you can turn around and re-set for your next repetition. This is a tricky one and a lesson in 'take what you are given'. If your starting point is your dog's foot just touching yours, great, reinforce that and build on from there. Practise until your dog is fluently returning to the Peek-A-Boo position and targeting your foot with theirs, in order for you to say, 'Good' and to then treat.

3. Cue 'PEEK-A-BOO' but this time use your treat to lure their head into a position that allows <u>each</u> of their two front feet to target <u>each</u> of your feet. When in place, feed your dog several individual treats so they can get used to being comfortable when standing on your feet, say, 'Good' and toss a treat out front for them to go and get.

Easy Peasy Ponder Points

🐾 In order of preference, list the three most appropriate pairs of shoes you can wear to do this exercise (remember, Crocs are never appropriate)

1. ....

2. ....

3. ....

🐾 Does luring your dog's head to the right help them raise and place their left foot correctly? And vice versa?

....

🐾 What else have you discovered helps your dog to make the desired foot placement?

....

🐾 Has enthusiasm and fun been maintained?

....

🐾 Is your cue still being given consistently?

....

What was good?

....
....
....

What could be better?

....
....
....

What will you do to improve?

....
....
....

Easy Peasy
Pearl of Wisdom:
TREATS

Hands up whose dog loves food?

Thought so!

The use of food, or treats, in dog training just cannot be beaten for effectiveness. Food is what's known as a 'primary reinforcer', one of the big-hitters in the canine 'feel-good' stakes. Of course, toys, play, affection and praise all have their place, but for teaching new behaviours, treats are hard to beat!

In addition to your dog's daily food allowance, food really should be used in training to accelerate your progress through all exercises. Food can also be used to help your dog relax and to offer additional enrichment to their daily routines.

Make sure you keep an eye on your dog's daily calorie intake, adjust meal portions to account for the extra goodies your dog receives constructively elsewhere throughout the day.

There's a whole range of treats available for dogs on the market. Some are healthier than others, so always read the label to ensure you're avoiding any dietary nasties. Personally, my dogs adore lamb and fish treats and, in addition, they swoon in the wake of my culinary genius as I manage, with the skill of a 10-star Michelin chef, to cut things into cubes!

Treats for Training

When using treats for training (and you really should!), make sure the treats are small, quickly consumed, high value and not too messy for you to handle. The *small and quickly consumed* aspect is really important. Don't want to use a treat that's so chewy or takes so long to eat that by the time your dog has swallowed it, they've forgotten what they did to earn it in the first place!

Each dog will have their own preference but try some of these to see which treats most floats your dog's boat:

- chicken slices
- sliced frankfurters
- beef jerky
- cheese cubes
- luncheon meat
- ham slices

Admittedly, the above aren't the healthiest, but they are fine in moderation, and let's be honest, for something to be a treat, it has to be, well . . . a treat!

You never know, you may find your dog prefers some of these healthier options:

- apple
- carrot
- banana

- celery
- fish treats
- blueberries

I've worked with a dog in the past who would smash though a brick wall to get to a piece of mange tout. Each to their own!

Enjoy the process of trial and error. Spend a bit of quality time to find out what your dog enjoys the most and don't be afraid to mix up 3–4 different treats in your training pouch before a session to keep things interesting. Not only will different flavours and textures appeal, but also the way you deliver the treat will have an effect.

If you don't want your dog to grab, make sure you bring the treat *to* your dog's mouth, to avoid them having to reach and snap.

If you want to add more speed, excitement and urgency to the exercise, try rolling the treat along the floor for your dog to chase.

Treats for Chillin'

Apart from the chomping noises, my house is at its quietest when each of the dogs are chilling out with a nice carrot or celery stick to kick back and gnaw upon.

Unfortunately, some foods are dangerous for dogs to eat, so definitely avoid the following:

- onions
- chocolate
- Xylitol (present in products such as chewing gum and sweets)
- Macadamia nuts
- grapes
- avocado

If you REALLY want to go up in your dog's estimation, pop on your apron and give my homemade **Easy Peasy Liver Cake** a go:

Ingredients:
450g lamb or ox liver *
450g self-raising flour **
4 eggs
100ml water

* to change it up, swap the liver for sardine
**for a less crumbly mix, use rice flour. (How do I know this stuff?! Move over, Gordon and Jamie!)

1. Turn oven to 180°C degrees.
2. Blend the liver (or sardines) in a food processor.
3. Whisk the eggs and water together.
4. Add the flour to the egg mixture and stir until smooth.

5. Mix everything together and pour mixture into a greased baking tray and bake for approximately 45 minutes.
6. Allow to cool then cut into small pieces.
7. Keep in fridge or freezer.
8. Prepare to be the local dog park rock star!

On a scale of 1 to 10, how much does your dog love their treats?

....

On a scale of 1 to 10, how much do you want your dog to love your training sessions together?

....

On a scale of 1 to 10, how crazy would you need to be not to use treats in training?

....

WEEK 29

Look To Say

Please #3

Challenge: Look To Say Please #3

The Target: Asking Politely

You bought my book! This means you're one of the good guys! Because of that, I don't want . . .

- 🐾 Your arm pulled out of your socket when your dog wants to run off to play with other dogs. I'd like them to look at you to say, 'Please can I go play?'
- 🐾 Your dog to 'mug' you when you enter the room with their food bowl. I'd like them to look at you to say, 'Please put my food down for me.'
- 🐾 Your dog scratching the back door because they want to go out. I want them to look at you to say, 'Please can you open the door for me?'

Frustration from dogs, toddlers and Brits abroad raises its ugly head when they don't know how to access something they want. Our concept of Look To Say Please will take that weight of frustration from their shoulders by showing them how to ask for access to what they want. Politely and quietly!

The Training

1. With your dog on the lead, stand still together as you throw a treat 3 metres in front of the pair of you.

2. Your dog will watch the flight of the treat and when it lands, they'll try to mind-Jedi the treat from the ground into their mouth. When that doesn't work, they'll go back into their memory bank to ask themselves, What behaviour gave me access to the treats last time?

3. Here's where your patience needs to stay strong: say nothing, and no sneaky body movements to try and catch your dog's eye! Just wait. The split-second they glance up towards you, say, 'Good!' and the pair of your run out together so that your dog can find and enjoy the treat.

4. As you progress, step behind your dog once you've thrown the treat. Now your dog will need to make a real concerted effort to look over their shoulder, away from the treat and towards you. That's a tough ask, but you can do it!

Easy Peasy Ponder Points

🐾 What's the best distance for you to throw the treat in order to get quicker Eye Contact?

....

🐾 What else does your dog love that you could throw? (A party?)

....

Name 5 other places you can practise this week.

1. ....
2. ....
3. ....
4. ....
5. ....

What was good?

....
....
....
....

What could be better?

....
....
....
....

What will you do to improve?

....
....
....
....

Doggy Diary

Write down all the amazing things you did
with your dog this week!

Monday and Tuesday

....

....

....

Wednesday and Thursday

....

....

....

Friday

....

....

....

Saturday and Sunday

....

....

....

WEEK 30

Supersonic Sits

#3

Challenge: Supersonic Sits #3

The Target: Building duration

By now you should be willing to bet good money that when you say, 'Sit' (and just once), regardless of location and position, your dog will drop anchor with the urgency of a drunk dad playing musical chairs. However, it's no good getting your dog to sit if they then leg it before you can get to them to pop the lead back on! Now's the time to introduce Duration into the proceedings. In other words, 'Sit means Sit, until I ask you what else to do next . . .'

The Training

1. Ask for a Sit, count to 5 seconds with your dog maintaining their position, then say, 'Good' and reinforce by rolling a treat or toy for your dog to chase and enjoy.

2. After each successful repetition, add an extra 5 seconds to the next attempt. If your dog wiggles or breaks position before you say, 'Good', no bother at all. Just go back to a 1-second duration and build up a second at a time after each successful attempt. When you get to 10 seconds, start building in blocks of 5 seconds.

3. Remember to keep *proofing*. Dog on your left, dog on your right, in front and behind. Use your imagination and get creative with your set-ups (if they're impressive, email me a pic!). Your mission, should you wish to accept it, is to aim for a solid Sit for 2 minutes, 3 times in a row. One with your dog on your left, one with your dog on your right and one with your back to your dog. If you can think of any other weird positions, go for it, but don't blame me if you end up at the chiropractor!

Easy Peasy Ponder Points

🐾 Are your raises in criteria smooth and realistic? (Hint: your dog's performance will tell you.)

....

🐾 Could you practise in a wider variety of locations?

....

🐾 Are you saying, 'Good' *before* producing the reinforcement?

....

🐾 Are you enjoying the training?

....

🐾 How can you reinforce *yourself* for a job well done? (Cake works for me!)

....

🐾 How can you introduce more Sits into your dog's daily routine?

....

🐾 Have you noticed a specific duration of time that your dog struggles to achieve?

....

🐾 How can you make the session more enjoyable for your dog?

....

What was good?

....
....
....

What could be better?

....
....
....

What will you do to improve?

....
....
....

Doggy Diary

Write down all the amazing things you did
with your dog this week!

Monday and Tuesday

....

....

....

Wednesday and Thursday

....

....

....

Friday

....

....

....

Saturday and Sunday

....

....

....

WEEK 31
The Magic Hand
Touch #3

Challenge: The Magic Hand Touch #3

The Target: Adding duration

You're now getting a super-reliable Hand Touch, and that's great, but I want you to really raise the bar by adding Duration to the behaviour. If we can get your dog to hold their nose to your hand for 5, 10 or even 30 seconds, you're going to have a really useful husbandry skill to help with grooming, vet inspections, ear cleaning and many more activities where a happy yet stationary dog will make life so much easier!

The Training

1. Produce your hand, say, 'Touch', count 1 second of nose contact, say, 'Good' and reinforce.

2. Produce your hand, say, 'Touch', count 2 seconds of nose contact, say, 'Good' and reinforce.

3. Produce your hand, say, 'Touch', count 5 seconds of contact, say, 'Good' and reinforce.

4. Play with the duration of contact prior to saying 'Good'; sometimes raise the bar, sometimes lower it, follow a 10-second Touch with a 2-second one.

5. Funk it up a little by saying, 'Touch' but slowly walking away from your dog so they're chasing you to make nose contact.

6. Maybe circle your hand or turn on your toes to encourage your dog to make contact, even when you're both on the move. This will help with about-turns should you see a danger ahead when out and about.

Easy Peasy Ponder Points

🐾 What's the furthest distance you can cue your dog to come and do a Hand Touch from?

....

🐾 Does luring your dog's head to the right help them raise and place their left foot correctly? And vice versa?

....

🐾 Are there any obstacles on your daily walk that you can cue your dog over, such as a stile, a kissing gate or an exhausted jogger?

....

🐾 Can you encourage your dog to crawl under a chair or table to do a Hand Touch?

....

🐾 What's the longest Duration of Hand Touch that you and your dog can perform today?

....

What was good?

....
....
....
....

What could be better?

....
....
....
....

What will you do to improve?

....
....
....
....

TIP: to help with Duration, when your dog touches your hand, maintain the contact but softly move your hand away from your dog so they can get used to pushing their nose into you. That'll help you add a few important seconds to your Duration target.

Doggy Diary

Write down all the amazing things you did with your dog this week!

Monday and Tuesday

....

....

....

Wednesday and Thursday

....

....

....

Friday

....

....

....

Saturday and Sunday

....

....

....

WEEK 32
The Smiling Lead
#3

Challenge: The Smiling Lead #3

The Target: The Great Outdoors

Now's the time to go public with your Smiling Lead!

I don't want your dog to practise pulling on the lead, so if your park is a fair distance from your home, either drive there (with your dog!), or pop them in the 'other' harness and bandana that allows them to pull. When they're in the *pulling* harness and bandana, there's no opportunity for them to earn treats, but if they're pulling then you're not allowed to sulk either! That's the discipline I talked about!

When you're both ready, have them in their appropriate harness, remove the bandana if necessary and . . .

The Training

1. Stand still, drop a treat, let them have it, and another . . . then stop dropping . . .

2. As soon as your dog looks to you, say, 'Good!' and reinforce **on the move**, as before. This time, however, be aware that you're in a much more difficult and distracting environment. Walk nice and slowly, keep changing direction and *pay well*!

3. After 2 or 3 minutes of you reinforcing your dog for Eye Contact on the move, give yourself a break. Maybe sit on the floor and give your dog a well-deserved belly rub, or pull out their favourite toy for a bit of playtime.

4. When you're ready, start your on-lead walking together again, but this time change it up a little: change pace, go a few more steps in the one direction before turning, see if you can manage 3–4 steps of Eye Contact on the move before saying, 'Good!' and reinforcing.

5. Keep the sessions short but increase your distance or duration of Eye Contact before treating. If your dog glances away, that's perfectly acceptable, it's the slack lead that we're wanting, so if there's a 'smile' in the lead as the pair of you are walking together, you've cracked it!

Easy Peasy Ponder Points

🐾 Are your expectations realistic? The park is so much more distracting than your garden, you know! Set out your (realistic!) expectations here:

....

....

🐾 Don't make sudden changes of direction or pace to *test* your dog. Give them every chance to succeed, you're on the same side. How are you helping your dog?

....

🐾 Is your lead nice and long to allow for 'slack'? About 2 metres is ideal.

....

🐾 Don't be too greedy. If you feel the standard is deteriorating or your discipline is waning, stop, play a game, chill out, make the most of your time together and then head home. Tomorrow's another day. What games can you play to lighten the mood?

....

What was good?

....

....

....

....

What could be better?

....

....

....

....

What will you do to improve?

....

....

....

....

Easy Peasy
Pearl of Wisdom:
HEAT

What is heatstroke?

Heatstroke is when your dog's body temperature rises so high that they're unable to bring it back down to a safe level. A dog's normal temperature is 38.3°C to 39.2°C, but it only takes a rise of 2°C or 3°C in a matter of minutes to generate excessive heat that can very quickly begin to damage the dog's organs, causing severe damage.

Let's be blunt with the worrying medical facts here: only 50% of dogs diagnosed with heatstroke survive.

Worst of all – **a dog can die from heatstroke in** *15 minutes.*

Things to do on a hot day to avoid heatstroke

- Ensure fresh water is readily available.
- Go out very early or very late in the day for exercise to avoid high temperatures.
- Provide a paddling pool for your dog to enjoy.
- Offer plenty of cool, shady areas for your dog to literally chill!
- Never leave your dog in a car, caravan or conservatory on a hot day.
- Check the pavement temperature before walking your dog. If it's too hot for you to place your hand on it for 5 seconds, it's definitely too hot for your dog's feet!

- Be aware that artificial grass can become twice as hot as natural grass on a hot day.
- Take responsibility. Don't assume your dog will decide themselves to slow down if they start to get hot.
- Keep walk durations shorter. So, 2 or 3 shorter walks are better than one long hot expedition.
- Know the weather forecast and plan your day accordingly.

Learn to spot the signs of heatstroke

- Glazed, panicked eyes
- Fast heart beat
- Muscle tremors
- Heavy panting
- Vomiting
- High body temperature
- Bright red tongue
- Lethargic
- Distressed
- Dark red or pale gums
- Weak legs, collapse
- Dribbling or foaming at the mouth

Your dog may be particularly at risk from heatstroke if they are:

- Under 12 months of age
- Elderly
- A giant breed such as a St Bernard, Newfoundland or Bernese Mountain Dog
- A breed with a heavy coat such as a Huskie or Chow Chow
- A Brachycephalic (flat-faced) breed, such as a Pug, Boston terrier or any type of Bulldog

What to do if you suspect heatstroke

- Call your emergency vet.
- Place your dog on top of wet towels, in the shade, by a fan.
- Offer your dog a little *room-temperature* drinking water.
- Massage your dog's legs to improve circulation.
- Apply room-temperature water to your dog's underarms, chest and pads.

YOUR DOG

WON'T ALWAYS KNOW
WHAT YOU'RE SAYING

BUT THEY'LL ALWAYS KNOW

HOW YOU
MAKE THEM

Feel!

WEEK 33

The Seek Back

#3

Challenge: The Seek Back #3

The Target: 'Shirt Button' drops

It's time to shift your Seek Backs up a gear. Rather than one item per Seek Back, you're going to make multiple drops . . . and hopefully multiple finds!

The Training

1. First, fill three small Tupperware boxes with your dog's favourite treats.

2. Walk with your dog beside you, drop a box as before and continue your stroll. After a further 10 or so strides, drop another box. Keep on walking and when you're ready, drop the third box and again keep on walking . . .

3. After several steps, do an about-turn, ask your dog to 'Find It!' and begin your search . . .

4. After finding the first box, drop to your knees, excitedly open the lid and feed your dog. Once done, pop the box into your pocket, stand up and excitedly say to your dog, 'Wanna find another buddy? C'mon then! FIND IT!' as the pair of you go on the hunt for box number two . . .

5. After successfully finding and enjoying the treasure of box number two, you've guessed it, go find box three together!

Easy Peasy Ponder Points

🐾 Are your Seek Backs better on-lead or off-lead at the moment?

....

....

🐾 What would make off-lead Seek Backs easier?

....

....

....

🐾 What's your dog's Top 3 box contents?

1. ....

2. ....

3. ....

🐾 How many Seek Backs will you do per daily walk this week?

....

....

....

What was good?

....

....

....

....

What could be better?

....

....

....

....

What will you do to improve?

....

....

....

....

Doggy Diary

Write down all the amazing things you did with your dog this week!

Monday and Tuesday

....

....

....

Wednesday and Thursday

....

....

....

Friday

....

....

....

Saturday and Sunday

....

....

....

WEEK 34
Total Recalls
#3

Challenge: Total Recalls #3

The Target: Adding Distraction

Now that your dog clearly knows what 'COME!' means to them, and you're getting the desired behaviour of your dog running to you when you call, it's time to raise the bar and maintain the same response, but with a little more temptation in the way!

Be confident: the pair of you can do this!

The Training

1. In a safe area, pop the normal lead on your dog's harness and have one of their toys in your pocket. Take the toy and throw it 5 metres in front of you. Stand still, holding your dog's lead. Your dog will turn away from you and look towards where you've thrown the toy, wanting to investigate and play together.

2. Stand your ground, say nothing. Be patient. ONLY when your dog turns their face towards you, excitedly say, 'COME!', jog back a few paces and as soon as your dog commits to running towards you happily, say, 'Good!' and run back with your dog towards the toy for a play. This one's tricky! We're asking your dog to look away from the toy and run in the opposite direction towards you, in order for them to get the toy!

3. Once you can do several repetitions smoothly and with continuous success, you can again raise the bar by using an even more tempting toy and by throwing it a shorter distance from you. Warning: the closer the toy, the stronger its magnetism! If you experience a few sticky repetitions and it's a real struggle for your dog to look or run towards you, don't sweat it, just throw the toy further away so its invisible magnetic force-field is not so potent!

4. When your dog is reliably looking to you as soon as you throw the toy, then upgrade from a toy to a treat. When you've mastered a Recall to you **away** from a tempting treat, throw a whole Tupperware box of the stuff away from you. That'll give you plenty to work on!

Easy Peasy Ponder Points

🐾 Try jogging backwards when you Recall your dog. What difference does it make to your dog's speed and enthusiasm?

....

🐾 Recall is a team game and I want to associate your presence with the celebration and reinforcement. What rewards can you use to ensure you stay part of the celebration?

....

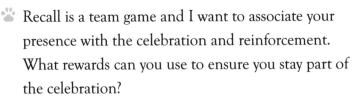

🐾 Go at your dog's pace. For the next ten times that you call your dog, make a note of the number of occasions that your dog instantly turned and *ran* to you.

....

What was good?

....

....

....

....

What could be better?

....

....

....

....

What will you do to improve?

....

....

....

....

Doggy Diary

Write down all the amazing things you did with your dog this week!

Monday and Tuesday

....

....

....

Wednesday and Thursday

....

....

....

Friday

....

....

....

Saturday and Sunday

....

....

....

WEEK 35

Detection Dog

#3

Challenge: Detection Dog #3

The Target: The Target Scent: True Detection

By now, both you and your dog know what to do when you say 'Find It'. You've reinforced the *searching* with a *find* and then reinforced the *find* with a *treat*.

Now let's get advanced. I want to show you how to teach your dog skills that I train with real working detection dogs: you're going to teach your dog to search and find a **target scent** other than food. Don't be at all intimidated! I don't care what breed of dog you have, you can do this!

In preparation, I want you to grab a few cotton wool balls, pop a couple of drops of clove oil, gun oil or birch oil onto each ball and keep them together, sealed in a large jar.

You've put all of your effort into getting the correct Indication behaviour on treats, now it's time to become a true detection dog handler and get the Indication on a *specific target scent*.

The Training

1. Go back and take a seat in your original chair, where you first introduced the concept of 'Find It'. However, this time, rather than having the single treat-loaded pot in your hand behind your back, have a pot containing one of the scent-infused cotton wool balls.

2. Once you take a seat and pop your hands behind your back, your dog will think, *Ah, this seems familiar, I know what's coming next!*

3. As soon as you bring the hand holding the **target scent** pot around to the front, your dog will sniff it – as soon as they do, say, 'Good!', remove the pot and give them a few treats from your pocket. Repeat several times so your dog learns that sniffing the **target scent** pays really well!

4. Now offer two pots from behind your back, one with the target scent in, the other pot empty. Allow your dog to sniff one pot and when their nose lands on the target scent, Bingo! . . . say, 'Good' and reinforce. Behind your back, swap the pots around in your hands so you know your dog is definitely identifying the **target scent**, not just guessing the hand!

5. When your dog sniffs the **target scent**, wait a few seconds to add some duration to the Indication, prior to saying, 'Good' and treating.

6. As with DETECTION DOG #2, you're now ready to place the target scent pot under a saucepan, hidden among a few other dummy pans.

7. Mix up the pan layout so your dog gets an opportunity of a good search before indicating the hidden treasure!

8. To really test your skills, you and your dog can go out of the room and have someone else hide the target pot before you and your detection dog get called to the scene to investigate!

Easy Peasy Ponder Points

🐾 Can you see evidence of learning?

....

🐾 Are you handling your target scent like a Pro to avoid contamination?

....

....

🐾 Are you clearly saying 'Good' *before* moving for your treats?

....

....

🐾 Could your treats be better? Be honest, ask your dog!

....

....

🐾 Are you seeing your dog's body language change when they discover the target scent?

....

....

What was good?

....

....

....

....

What could be better?

....

....

....

....

What will you do to improve?

....

....

....

....

Doggy Diary

Write down all the amazing things you did with your dog this week!

Monday and Tuesday

....

....

....

Wednesday and Thursday

....

....

....

Friday

....

....

....

Saturday and Sunday

....

....

....

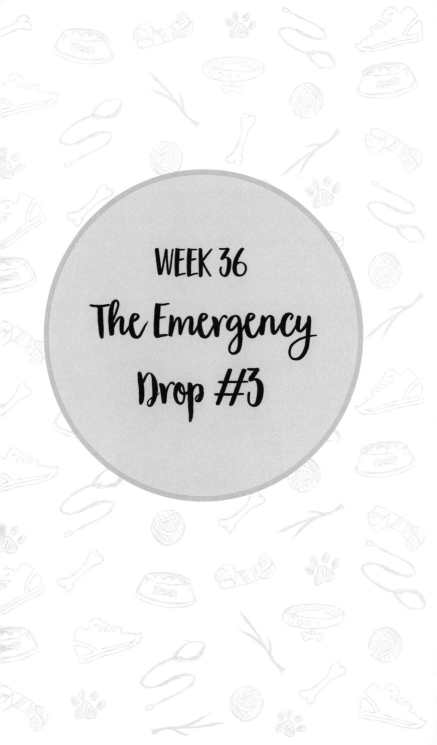

WEEK 36
The Emergency
Drop #3

Challenge: The Emergency Drop #3

The Target: 'Drop' to release

With all the seeds of the Emergency Drop now planted, it's time to actually start to get the behaviour of your dog opening their mouth to release an item when given the cue to Drop.

The Training

1. Grab a 12-inch length of hosepipe or rolled up tea-towel. Sit or kneel, facing your dog.

2. From behind your back, slowly bring the hosepipe to the front on the floor and as soon as your dog puts their mouth to the hosepipe say, 'Drop', then, with your hand still on the stationary pipe, bring a treat with your other hand from your treat pouch to the front and place on the floor for your dog. Once the first treat has been eaten, throw the second treat for your dog to chase as you return the hosepipe to behind your back.

3. Bring the hosepipe to the front and, with short movements, entice your dog to put their mouth onto it. As soon as your dog puts their mouth onto the hosepipe, say, 'Drop'. Hold the hosepipe stationary, repeat the treat steps as above, and return the hosepipe to behind your back.

4. Bring the hosepipe to the front, allow your dog to place their mouth on it for longer and make some slow, gentle movements to keep your dog engaged with the game. After 5 seconds, hold the hosepipe dead still, say, 'Drop', then repeat the treat steps as above.

5. The pair of you should then play tuggy with the hosepipe, but after a few seconds <u>you</u> let go, then say, 'Drop'. If your dog drops, reinforce them as before, then bang on next-door neighbour's door to tell them who's got the bestest dog!

Easy Peasy Ponder Points

🐾 Can you still get a reliable drop after 5 seconds tugging? How about after 10 seconds tugging? How about after 20 seconds tugging?

....

🐾 List 5 other items you can play tuggy with during your Drop sessions:

1. ....

2. ....

3. ....

4. ....

5. ....

🐾 When you stop the game prior to saying, 'Drop', what's the best height to 'freeze' the toy at, to give you the best chance of a clean drop?

....

🐾 Is there a difference between holding the toy to the floor, versus holding it at your dog's eye level?

....

🐾 Other than treats, how else could you reinforce a good Drop?

....

What was good?

....

....

What could be better?

....

....

What will you do to improve?

....

....

Easy Peasy
Pearl of Wisdom:
MOTIVATION AND
LIFE REWARDS

Without Motivation, there simply isn't any behaviour! I'd describe Motivation as: *a reason for behaving in a particular way to achieve a desired consequence.*

Let's face it: if you do a particular behaviour and, as a consequence, you receive something pretty damn cool, you're going to be keen to do that behaviour again. Same with dogs!

We're fans of positive reinforcement at Easy Peasy HQ, so the reason we want your dog to do a <u>behaviour</u> when you ask them to, is so that they can <u>achieve a desired consequence</u> that they find reinforcing.

From your dog's perspective, when you ask them to do a certain behaviour, a desired consequence may be:

- A great belly rub!
- A cube of cheese
- A game of tug

Or it may be a Life Reward such as:

- Jumping in the car for a road trip
- Going out of the front door for a great walk with you
- Being let off the lead to go-play with other dogs

A great way to motivate your dog is to discover what consequences *they desire*, and to use those consequences to reinforce the behaviours *you desire!*

Don't listen to all the nonsense that your dog isn't behaving because, 'They're stubborn' or 'They're trying to dominate you.' There's really only 3 reasons your dog won't do what you're asking them to do:

- They're physically unable to it.

  Don't ask a Chihuahua to change a light bulb

- They don't understand what you're asking them to do.

  You haven't yet taught them properly what the cue means

- They're not motivated enough.

  If it's worth it to them, of course they'll do it!

Before your next training session, tip the cards in your favour by writing down a list of potential consequences below, and figuring out how you can use each of them to get the behaviours you want from your dog, when you ask for them:

List 3 treats your dog adores that you could use to reinforce a Sit, a Down and a Hand Touch:

1. ....
2. ....
3. ....

List 3 novel ways you can deliver those foods:

1. ....
2. ....
3. ....

List 5 games you can play with your dog to reinforce a Recall, a Seek Back and a Boomerang:

1. ....
2. ....
3. ....
4. ....
5. ....

List 5 activities you can give your dog access to in order to reinforce Look To Say Please, The Smiling Lead and Hit the Brakes:

1. ....
2. ....
3. ....
4. ....
5. ....

One final point about Motivation: think about what your particular breed was bred to do. What types of behaviour just make your dog feel like a million dollars? Perhaps you've got a Gundog? Maybe they adore carrying things in their mouth. Perhaps you've a Terrier with hundreds of years of wiring that's tapped into their love of shaking and ragging 'toys'? You may live with a herding breed, a character that adores the opportunity to control and gather in tennis balls for you?

So always consider the breed but, more importantly, consider the individual in front of you. Look at them now. What would they love to do with you *right now*? How can you use that activity in order to reinforce the behaviours you'd like your dog to do, so you're both winners?

WEEK 37
Hit The Brakes
#3

Challenge: Hit The Brakes #3

The Target: Building Duration

You've smashed the first two important elements of Hit the Brakes: firstly, what it *means to your dog* and secondly, getting the behaviour *you* want. At this stage, we're going to concentrate on building the *duration* of the behaviour, that is, the time between your dog doing the behaviour of 'Stop', and them getting the treat. By building the duration, you can be safe in the knowledge that your dog will stop – and *stay* stopped – until you ask them for the next behaviour you want them to do, or you reinforce them for a job well done.

Remember the dog that was about to run back into the oncoming traffic? The fact that the owner had taught the dog to Stop with duration gave that person the opportunity to safely cross the road and pop the lead onto her dog, without the dog breaking from their stationary position.

That's how important the following steps are . . .

The Training

1. With the correct body language, hand and verbal signal, say, 'Stop'. Wait until your dog freezes, count 1 second then, rather than tossing the treat behind their butt, I want you to walk forward and feed your dog in the position they're stood in. Importantly, by feeding in position, your dog will learn to 'stay put' and wait for you to come to them when they Stop. This will help you build duration and also discourage your dog from sneaking forward to get the goodies from you.

2. With your dog 5–10 metres away from you, say, 'Stop!', this time count to 5 seconds before going to them as they stand in their stationary position, waiting for you to pay them.

3. Following each successful repetition, add a little more distance between you and your dog before giving the cue, and add a little more duration between getting the behaviour and walking to your dog to reinforce them in position.

4. Don't be too proud to go back a few steps for distance or duration if you see your dog moving after you've given the cue. Don't get greedy!

Easy Peasy Ponder Points

🐾 Still consistent with your body language? Note down any thoughts you have on that.

....

🐾 Maybe it's time to introduce a ball as the reinforcer to reward your dog for a great Hit the Brakes in a slightly more exciting state? Anything else you could introduce?

....

🐾 If all is going well, could you practise safely in a more distracting environment?

....

🐾 Are you being honest with your criteria, not asking for too much too soon?

....

What was good?

....

....

....

....

What could be better?

....

....

....

....

What will you do to improve?

....

....

....

....

Doggy Diary

Write down all the amazing things you did with your dog this week!

Monday and Tuesday

....

....

....

Wednesday and Thursday

....

....

....

Friday

....

....

....

Saturday and Sunday

....

....

....

WEEK 38
Say Your Prayers
#3

Challenge: Say Your Prayers #3

The Target: The Head Drop

Now that you've put in the work and you're smoothly getting two front feet up onto the platform, it's time to get your dog to drop their head nice and low, so they can pray with sincerity.

The Training

1. Say your cue 'Target' and encourage your dog to place their two front feet onto the platform. When in position, hold a treat under your dog's nose and slowly lure their head down 5cm towards the platform's surface. As soon as your dog drops their head, say, 'Good' and give them the treat.

2. Following each successful repetition of the above, lure your dog's head an extra 5cm lower before saying, 'Good' and reinforcing with the treat.

3. The final position is to lure your dog's chin to lay flat on the platform, resting between their two front feet.

4. When nice and reliable, encourage your dog onto the platform with a 'Target' and when their two feet are in position, say, 'Prayers' and lure their head down between their feet. Amen!

Easy Peasy Ponder Points

🐾 Which seems easier to lure, the first 5cm drop of the head, or the final 5cm drop of the head to the platform?

....

....

....

🐾 Will your dog now get into position on the platform with just a verbal cue of 'Target' and 50% less luring?

....

....

....

🐾 Can you see any evidence of your dog learning what the cue 'Prayers' means?

....

....

....

What was good?

....

....

....

....

What could be better?

....

....

....

....

What will you do to improve?

....

....

....

....

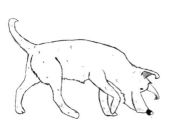

Doggy Diary

Write down all the amazing things you did with your dog this week!

Monday and Tuesday

....
....
....

Wednesday and Thursday

....
....
....

Friday

....
....
....

Saturday and Sunday

....
....
....

WEEK 39
Rock Around
The Clock #3

Challenge: Rock Around The Clock #3

The Target: Shifting The Perspective

You've done brilliantly so far!

You can leave a treat on the bowl, stand behind your dog then call your dog AWAY from the treat. Shut up! The pair of you are amazing!

Now it's time to maintain those core behaviours of Sit, Eye Contact, Recall and Touch, but to change the context (and temptation!) by you working your way around the clock face.

The Training

1. If you and your dog are scoring 10 out of 10 with your dog sat at 6 o'clock, then do the same set-up, but return to **7 o'clock** once you've placed a treat on the bowl. Recall and Hand Touch from your new location.

2. Next, leave your dog in a Sit a '6', load a treat onto the bowl, then Recall and Hand Touch from **8 o'clock**.

3. Finally, ask your dog to Sit at '6', pop the treat on the bowl then step over to the **9 o'clock** on the dial. You and your dog will now be forming a right-angle with a very tempting treat at the centre spot of the dial!

4. With every ounce of joy you can muster, call your dog . . . (*crosses fingers*) . . . if your dog runs directly to you, WOW! Get your Hand Touch, say, 'Good!' and run over to the bowl with your dog to enjoy the goodies. If your dog doesn't, then relax in the knowledge that they're smart and they'll probably survive okay in the wild without you, if needs be! Simply head back to 6 o'clock, and build up again from there. Enjoy the journey!

Easy Peasy Ponder Points

🐾 As you work your own body position around the clock face from 7 to 9 o'clock, the temptation for your dog to grab the treat rather than Recall becomes greater and greater. What body language have you seen from your dog that they're contemplating a sneaky smash-and-grab before Recalling?

....

🐾 What stage of Around the Clock has proved the trickiest to achieve so far?

....

🐾 Try 2 different treats. Do you notice any difference in your dog's performance?

Treat 1:

....

Difference:

....

Treat 2:

....

Difference:

....

🐾 Any difference in success rate if you use a beloved toy rather than treats?

....

🐾 How many times have you relied on the long line to prevent a fail?

....

🐾 What could you do to enable more success?

....

🐾 What effect does the location have on your training?

....

🐾 On a scale of 1 to 10, how confident are you that you'll be able to get your dog to Recall OVER a slice of ham to get to you?

....

What was good?

....

What could be better?

....

What will you do to improve?

....

Doggy Diary

Write down all the amazing things you did with your dog this week!

Monday and Tuesday

....

....

....

Wednesday and Thursday

....

....

....

Friday

....

....

....

Saturday and Sunday

....

....

....

WEEK 40

Boomerangs

#4

Challenge: Boomerangs #4

The Target: Drive On The Other Side

Hopefully by now there's NOTHING you can't Boomerang your dog around!

The final piece of the puzzle is to be able to send your dog from either side of you, and for them to be able to Boomerang both clockwise and anti-clockwise. This is known as teaching your dog to 'Drive On The Other Side'. By being an Ambidextrous Boomeranger©, not only will you keep your dog physically balanced and not biased to one side, you'll also have to up your game to make sure your handling is on-point!

The Training

1. Go back to your original object from page 9 and also back to 1 metre, but this time, with your dog on your *right-hand* side, you're going to cue the behaviour with your LEFT hand; and because everything is now going to be in reverse, your verbal cue is going to be REMOOB! (only kidding, stick with BOOMER).

2. It'll feel a little sticky and very different for your dog, but soon the penny will drop: you'll see another 'A-ha!' moment from your dog and you can then start increasing your distance, one step at a time.

3. Once you can safely 'Drive On The Other Side', introduce new objects to Boomerang around, and then you can start to Double-Up and focus on your footwork as you dance between the two objects!

Easy Peasy Ponder Points

🐾 What other exercises have you taught your dog predominantly on one side? (Revisit them and train from the opposite side.)

....

🐾 By changing sides and asking for a Boomerang, what percentage do you think your dog listens to your words for instruction, and what percentage do they look to your body language for clues?

....

....

🐾 With 5 attempts, what's the VERY furthest you can successfully send your dog around an object, clockwise AND anti-clockwise?

1. ....

2. ....

3. ....

4. ....

5. ....

What was good?

....

....

....

....

What could be better?

....

....

....

....

What will you do to improve?

....

....

....

....

Easy Peasy
Pearl of Wisdom:
PLAY

Humans and dogs are two of the very few mammals that continue to play long into adulthood. In addition to the pleasure principle, playing with your dog can also help to:

- 🐾 Build an amazing relationship
- 🐾 Teach your dog important social skills
- 🐾 Help you become fluent in each other's body language
- 🐾 Teach your dog how to behave, even when aroused and excited
- 🐾 Relieve stress, for you both!

With my dog-trainer's hat on, Play is also an excellent way to assess what kind of toys and games we can use when looking to reward the behaviours we want more of from our dog in the future. (It's not *all* about treats, you know!)

By suddenly freezing and successfully asking for a Sit mid-play before carrying on the fun antics, we're also teaching our dogs to listen and respond to our cues, even when they're super-excited and aroused. That can be a lifesaver in a real-life scenario.

By playing like a loon with your dog then successfully asking for a Down for 20 seconds before continuing the frenzy, you'll be helping your dog learn patience and self-control, plus increasing their frustration tolerance.

Play is not one type of behaviour. Some people love playing rugby, some love playing board games and some love to wrestle. Your dog will also have their own personal preferences when it comes to playing games with you. Consider a few of the suggestions below and just get on with it!

There's no *right* or *wrong*: if it's safe, you're both enjoying it and at least one of you is wearing clothes, then you're in business!

Play Suggestions

- **Play with sincerity**: Never think of Play sessions as a chore, or a task you need to tick off your 'To Do' list. Cut loose, turn off your phone, act the eejit and smile. You never know, 5 minutes of play with your dog may be the highlight of your day, as well as theirs.

- **If you can play with it, then it's a toy!** It's not so much about what the toy 'is', it's more about what the toy 'does'. Your dog definitely doesn't care how much you paid for it! Ignite the passion in your dog by twitching the toy along the floor like a little mouse. YOU act excited and impressed by the toy as you cradle it gently in your hands – dogs love a bit of monkey-see-monkey-do. If YOU love it, it must be worth checking out!

- 🐾 **Horses For Courses:** Don't be afraid to try a few different playing styles. Your dog may be a chaser, a tugger, a grabber, a catcher or a combination of all four. Only one way to find out!

- 🐾 **Hunting Play:** Get on your hands and knees and flick a knotted tea towel out in front of you and back in again to be shielded by your hand. With your dog's interest piqued, flick it out again and twitch it along the ground. As your dog pounces and grabs at the toy, gently make tiny jabbing movements to keep the toy 'alive' in your dog's mouth.

- 🐾 **Hide and Seek:** Sit on the floor with your left hand covering a treat. Randomly lift your covering hand and flick the treat along the floor for your dog to chase and grab. Reload, build suspense and flick again! Your dog's focus and interest in you will become intense!

- 🐾 **Peer Pressure:** When playing tuggy games, play with a strength and skill level similar to your dog's own.

- 🐾 **Swallow your pride:** Let your dog 'win' plenty of times. No one's interested in playing a game they know they'll lose every time!

- 🐾 **Every Day's a School Day:** Make a mental note of the toys and games your dog loves to play with

you. Use those games to reinforce the behaviours
you want more of during your training sessions.

Quality Time: Play *can* be high-octane, super-
physical and frenetic, but it doesn't have to be.
Meet your dog at the level they're at. Your dog
may be older, shy or just a naturally gentle soul.
Cool. With one of my dogs, our favourite game
is for me to pick a dandelion or daisy, hold it
in the air, then we both watch as it drops to
the ground. We can spend an hour doing that
and you know what, it only feels like 5 minutes
and when we're done, we're each fully relaxed
without a care in the world!

WEEK 41

Peek-A-Boo

#4

Challenge: Peek-A-Boo #4

The Target: Going mobile

Now that you can cue a 'Peek-A-Boo' and your dog can comfortably hold the position between your legs *and* place each of their front feet onto yours for 5 seconds, we can start to add a bit of movement, like when a dad teaches his young daughter how to dance at a wedding . . .

The Training

1. Cue your dog into the Peek-A-Boo position, with their feet on yours.

2. Slowly raise your toes on your right foot, leaving your heel in contact with the floor.

3. Repeat with your left foot. Don't rush it though otherwise you might end up in a bundle on the floor!

4. Take a tiny step forward with your right foot, and if your dog's foot remains on yours, treat in position.

5. Repeat with your left foot.

6. Progress by taking 2–3 steps before feeding your dog in position.

7. As confidence grows, increase the distance walked.

Easy Peasy Ponder Points

🐾 Could your initial steps be shorter?

....
....
....

🐾 Is your dog comfortable?

....
....
....

🐾 Do you sway when you walk?

....
....
....

🐾 Is your dog central between your legs?

....
....
....

What was good?

....

....

....

....

What could be better?

....

....

....

....

What will you do to improve?

....

....

....

....

Doggy Diary

Write down all the amazing things you did with your dog this week!

Monday and Tuesday

....

....

....

Wednesday and Thursday

....

....

....

Friday

....

....

....

Saturday and Sunday

....

....

....

WEEK 42

Look To Say

Please #4

Challenge: Look To Say Please #4

The Target: Real-life practice

Be proud of what you've achieved so far with your Eye Contact.

Now I want you to push the concept of Look To Say Please one final step, so you can use it in real-life scenarios to make you and your dog's lives less frustrating and also to open up the channels of communication to new, higher levels between the pair of you.

As a bonus feature, you are surrounded with natural opportunities to reinforce Eye Contact from your dog. I like to call these opportunities Life Rewards.

The Training

1. Get to the back door with your dog and stand with your fingers on the handle. As soon as your dog looks to you, say, 'Good', open the door, run out with your dog and have a great play session.

2. At walk time, pop the lead and harness onto your dog, stand by the front door and when your dog looks to you, say, 'Good', open the door and the pair of you enjoy your walk together.

3. During your walk, when you get to a kerbside, stop. When your dog looks up to you say, 'Good' and continue your stroll to the park.

4. In the middle of playing with your dog, hold the toy out to your side and twirl it around. As soon as your dog looks away from the toy and towards your eyes, say, 'Good!' and throw the toy again for them to chase.

Easy Peasy Ponder Points

🐾 List 5 other scenarios where you could reinforce Eye
Contact with something other than treats.

1. ....
2. ....
3. ....
4. ....
5. ....

🐾 What other exercises will become easier now your
dog looks to you?

....

....

....

....

🐾 In what ways and what circumstances does your dog
seem calmer, now that they know how to say 'Please'?

....

....

....

....

What was good?

....

....

....

....

What could be better?

....

....

....

....

What will you do to improve?

....

....

....

....

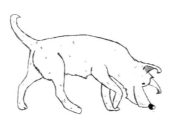

Doggy Diary

Write down all the amazing things you did with your dog this week!

Monday and Tuesday

....

....

....

Wednesday and Thursday

....

....

....

Friday

....

....

....

Saturday and Sunday

....

....

....

WEEK 43

Supersonic Sits

#4

Challenge: Supersonic Sits #4

The Target: The final piece of the puzzle: Distraction

You've already done the lion's share of the work to build a rock-solid Supersonic Sit for your dog. Nice one!

To ensure the exercise is as reliable as possible in as many situations as possible, you've already added plenty of Duration to account for real-life scenarios. On top of that, I now want your dog to be able to perform the behaviour of Sit, no matter what else is going on around you both.

This is where training and rehearsing with added Distraction comes in . . .

The Training

1. Ask your dog to Sit and then, with them maintaining their position, slowly bend down, untie then tie up your lace, stand upright, count for 5 seconds, say, 'Good' and treat your dog. If that was tricky, repeat, but move slower, don't bend so far, and perhaps pop your Velcro fastening shoes on for tomorrow's session!

2. Once the above step is reliable and you can achieve 5 out of 5, try the suggestions below to add more Distractions (and to freak out your neighbours!).

3. Ask for a Sit, and reinforce your dog if they stay in position, but while they Sit, I want you to:

   i. Jump up and down on the spot for 5 seconds.

   ii. Lay on the ground, face down, for 10 seconds.

   iii. Whistle your favourite TV theme music!

   iv. Toss a toy up and down in your hand for 20 seconds.

   v. Kiss a cat for an hour (joking!).

Easy Peasy Ponder Points

🐾 How can you add even more reliability?

....

🐾 Will it be beneficial for others to teach your dog
to Sit?

....

🐾 How can you use Life Rewards such as going into
the garden, being let off the lead and mealtimes to
reinforce your dog's Sit?

....

🐾 What can you do to make Sit training more fun?

....

🐾 Have you trained for the behaviour to be as reliable
outdoors as it is at home?

....

🐾 Ultimately, do you trust your dog to Sit when asked,
no matter the scenario?

....

What was good?

....

....

....

....

What could be better?

....

....

....

....

What will you do to improve?

....

....

....

....

Doggy Diary

Write down all the amazing things you did with your dog this week!

Monday and Tuesday

....
....
....

Wednesday and Thursday

....
....
....

Friday

....
....
....

Saturday and Sunday

....
....
....

WEEK 44
The Magic Hand
Touch #4

Challenge: The Magic Hand Touch #4

The Target: Husbandry skills

Let's get this show on the road!

You've done your homework so by now you'll have a really reliable Hand Touch on-cue, plus you've managed to get plenty of Duration so your dog will touch their nose to your hand and hold it there for a decent period of time before you say, 'Good' and treat.

Our final stage is to put the Hand Touch to good use to make your husbandry chores so much more pleasurable for you both.

The Training

1. Cue 'Touch' and when your dog's nose touches your hand, gently inspect their ears for 5 seconds, say, 'Good' to release the nose contact and reinforce with a treat.

2. Cue 'Touch' and when your dog's nose touches your hand, gently brush your dog's coat along their back for 5 seconds, say, 'Good' to release the nose contact and reinforce with a treat.

3. Cue 'Touch' and when your dog's nose touches your hand, pretend to administer eye drops to your dog for 5 seconds, say, 'Good' to release the nose contact, and reinforce.

4. Cue 'Touch' and when your dog's nose touches your hand, gently clip your lead on and off your dog 5 times, say, 'Good' to release the nose contact, and reinforce.

5. Repeat each of the above and increase the Duration over the session.

6. Repeat each of the above in a variety of locations.

Easy Peasy Ponder Points

🐾 List 5 useful applications of the Hand Touch.

1. ....
2. ....
3. ....
4. ....
5. ....

🐾 How could you use the Hand Touch to help your dog greet visitors politely?

....

🐾 What evidence do you have that your dog enjoys their Hand Touch training?

....

🐾 How could you use unclipping the lead, going outside, or other such Life Rewards to reinforce your Hand Touch?

....

What was good?

....

....

....

....

What could be better?

....

....

....

....

What will you do to improve?

....

....

....

....

Easy Peasy
Pearl of Wisdom:
VETS

They say that three things are inevitable in life: taxes, death and taking your dog to the vets. The good news is, your dog doesn't care about the first two and the third can be turned into a real treat!

First things first: choose the right vet. Ask around, take personal recommendations and if something doesn't feel right, move on and find another. Your vet is a vitally important player in the life of you and your dog. So, your choice will have a huge impact on your dog's stress levels and your peace of mind. Your vet should always have time to welcome and fully answer your questions, as well as demonstrate a real love of dogs and their well-being, both physically and mentally.

Make vet visits a positive

YOU have the power to make vet visits a positive and enjoyable activity for your dog. Build positive associations by simply popping in to your vet's surgery, asking the receptionist or vet nurse to give your dog a few treats, then leave. Do similar visits 2–3 times a week for a couple of weeks and your dog will be delighted the next time you go. By building that positive association, even if your dog needs some kind of procedure, they'll be starting from an optimistic position, therefore increasing their tolerance of being handled.

Know your dog's body language

If your dog knows that you 'listen' and respond appropriately when they ask you for help, they'll be so much more confident and relaxed going into the vet's surgery. Check out Body Language Pearl of Wisdom on page 141 for tips on what to look out for.

Fingers crossed it'll never happen, but in an emergency veterinary situation, your dog may be required to wear a muzzle. DON'T let that stressful emergency be the first time your dog is introduced to a muzzle. That'll only compound the stress. Make the investment now in a relaxed, unrushed manner, to introduce your dog to the **joy** of a muzzle. By investing that time **now**, you have the power to decide how your dog feels about a muzzle, positive or negative . . . your choice.

Of course, you want your dog to feel positive about a muzzle, so have a good look at the 'Hand Touch' mission (page 44), and once you've achieved all four stages, go back to stage one but rather than offering the palm of your hand for your dog to touch with their nose, offer the open muzzle in your hand for your dog to place their nose in (on their way to touching your hand); then build from there to eventually add your Duration and Distraction of securing the muzzle clips. See, it's almost as if I've planned this training for you!

Trigger Stacking

There are lots of little triggers involved in a vet visit that can all add up to massively increase your dog's stress level, if we're not careful. If you know a vet visit is in the diary, make sure your dog doesn't have any other stressors leading up to the visit. Keep events before your vet visit as relaxed and low-key as possible to make sure your dog still has plenty of tolerance left in their tank!

Manage the visit

There are a few simple preparation adjustments you can make prior to your vet visit that can keep your dog relaxed and happy. For example: avoid your dog getting over-aroused in the presence of other animals in the waiting room, so enter the premises without your dog to inform the receptionist of your arrival, and when the vet is ready to see you, perhaps you could bring your dog in via the back door to avoid walking past the menagerie of other patients. If your dog is not particularly comfortable in the small surgery, perhaps in the event of a simple veterinary procedure, your vet will be happy to see your dog in the practice's car park?

Be your dog's advocate: if there's any action you can take to make vet visits more comfortable for all concerned, then for the benefit of your dog, your vet and for you, please take that action double-quick.

Finally, here are a few of the Challenges that will make vet visits more pleasurable:

- SUPERSONIC SITS – will offer a familiar position and a positive association to the experience.
- HAND TOUCH – will help keep your dog stationary for inspections AND assist your muzzle training!
- PEEK-A-BOO – perfect to keep your dog safe and controlled in the waiting room and will make inspections so much easier.

WEEK 45
The Smiling Lead
#4

Challenge: The Smiling Lead #4

The Target: Alternative Reinforcers

You're doing great!

By now in your Smiling Lead career, you've definitely taught your dog that checking-in with you as the pair of you walk together is super-reinforcing. Bravo!

But even your dog knows, there's more to life than treats!

How else can you reinforce your dog for awesome Smiling Lead? What other Life Rewards are available?

The Training

Below are several opportunities to reinforce your dog for walking nicely on a smiling lead with you.

1. If your dog loves their walk (and whose dog doesn't?), when you get to a kerbside, stop, wait for your dog to glance up at you and when they do, say, 'Good!' and reinforce the Eye Contact by continuing your walk.

2. Walk through the park entrance with your dog on-lead. When the lead is loose between you, say, 'Good', unclip the harness and say, 'Off you go, buddy!' You've reinforced the loose-lead walking with the joy of some off-lead play.

3. Have your dog on-lead. Throw their favourite toy away from you. Wait for Eye Contact then slowly start walking together with a slack lead towards the toy. This is a real tempter though and where *your* discipline needs to be on-point. If the lead goes tight, just stop, stand still. When it's slack, slowly walk forward together for 10 steps then say, 'Good!' and the pair of you run off to find and play with the toy. If that goes well, then go for 15 steps tomorrow, then the day after, 20! Shut up! I know, right!

Easy Peasy Ponder Points

🐾 Make sure the Life Rewards on offer are genuinely
reinforcing for your dog's behaviour. Hint: It's not
about what your dog *should* love, it's about what they
do love!

....

....

🐾 Are you constantly on the lookout for Life Rewards
when you're with your dog? Don't miss an
opportunity.

....

....

....

🐾 What other reinforcement opportunities present
themselves to you when you're walking your dog?
Remember, where there's access to an activity your
dog loves, there's access to an opportunity to get the
behaviour from your dog that you love!

....

....

....

What was good?

....

....

....

....

What could be better?

....

....

....

....

What will you do to improve?

....

....

....

....

Doggy Diary

Write down all the amazing things you did with your dog this week!

Monday and Tuesday

....
....
....

Wednesday and Thursday

....
....
....

Friday

....
....
....

Saturday and Sunday

....
....
....

WEEK 46
The Seek Back
#4

Challenge: The Seek Back #4

The Target: Emergency Seek Backs!

Ever lost your keys?

Ever wished you'd taught your dog to find them?

You're welcome!

The Training

1. Walk with your dog, but this time, rather than dropping your treat pouch or other 'good news' items for your dog, drop your car keys. Don't break your stride (even though the inevitable 'chink' sound of your keys hitting the ground will be a Distraction!) . . .

2. After several strides, and exactly as you've rehearsed many times previously, guide your dog around, say, 'Find It!' and watch your dog go searching . . .

3. Have faith, dogs are curious creatures and the unique aroma of your metallic keys, covered in your own personal smell (no offence!), in contrast to the natural ground scent, will be enough for your dog to do a Scooby-Doo double-take when they catch a sniff of them on the air. YOU need to be super-quick here to notice that double-take and to encourage your dog to take you to the spot where your keys have landed.

4. As soon as the pair of you arrive at the keys, fall to your knees (you probably will anyway, overcome with relief!), and pretend to magic some treats from

underneath the keys to give to your dog. Here's where your sleight of hand is important again. If you can teach your dog that finding items in the park that have your scent on them are a source of reinforcement, then you'll never be locked out of your house ever again!

Easy Peasy Ponder Points

How many sessions did you have to do before you saw excitement and anticipation from your dog when they found the keys?

....

What other non-food personal items will you use this week for Seek Backs?

....

Other than food, how else can you reinforce a great Seek Back?

....

List 3 advantages for your dog to do Seek Backs:

1. ....

2. ....

3. ....

List 3 advantages for YOU for your dog to know how to do Seek Backs:

1. ....
2. ....
3. ....

What was good?

....
....
....
....

What could be better?

....
....
....
....

What will you do to improve?

....
....
....
....

Doggy Diary

Write down all the amazing things you did with your dog this week!

Monday and Tuesday

....
....
....

Wednesday and Thursday

....
....
....

Friday

....
....
....

Saturday and Sunday

....
....
....

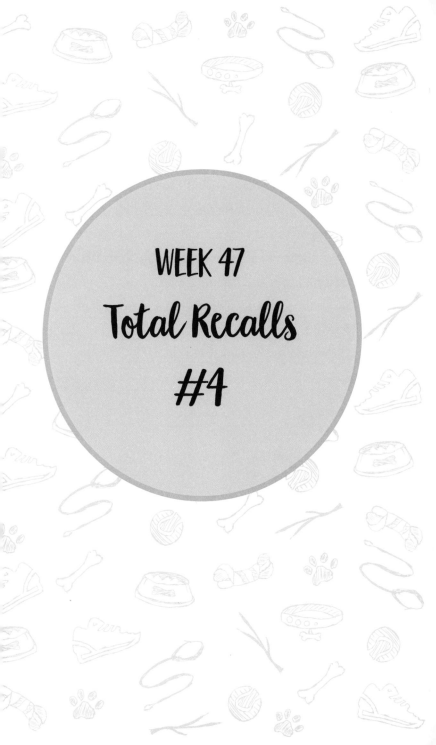

WEEK 47

Total Recalls

#4

Challenge: Total Recalls #4

The Target: Going 'Live'!

This is the final leg of our Recall training: you've done all of the hard work to condition what the cue of 'COME' means to your dog; you've reinforced your dog hundreds of times for running at speed to you; and you've successfully built a nice long history of Recalling your dog from the tempting Distraction of toys and treats.

Now it's time to put it all together and to go 'live'!

This is the big one: it's time to introduce your Recalls to your daily walks at the park. Eeeeek!

The Training

1. With the long line attached to your dog's harness, have a relaxed stroll with them in a quiet spot at the park. Say nothing for a good few minutes, then, as long as the line is slack between the pair of you, shout 'COME!', jog back a few steps and, as your dog runs towards you, praise heavily, drop a couple of treat-bombs their way and if their world revolves around a particular toy, produce that toy and go crazy for 30 seconds.

2. As you progress, get in the habit of throwing the treats or toys behind you or between your legs, (although NOT between your legs if you've got a Great Dane as you'll be riding your dog home backwards! Your Recall won't improve but you may get an audition for *Toy Story 5*!). I want you to toss the goodies behind you as that will encourage your dog to really accelerate and rush back towards you to get their reinforcement, rather than putting their brakes on as they get closer to you.

3. Over the coming weeks, follow each successful session with some Recalls in a slightly more distracting environment. If you hit an area that is just too tempting and the Recall performance isn't as on-point as you'd like, no biggie, it's just information on where you're training is at that time. Go back a few steps, heavily reinforce in a less distracting set-up to remind your dog of the game, then start to creep up the Distraction ladder again!

4. When you're confident, evolve towards having the long line trailing behind, then going completely off-lead. Don't rush it though, your dog's too precious: *safety first.*

Easy Peasy Ponder Points

🐾 Have you done everything you can to ensure you've both enjoyed the session?

....

🐾 Are you training at the correct pace, or asking too much too soon?

....

🐾 Are you only calling your dog when the long line is slack? We don't want any tension on the lead because that's uncomfortable for you both, but also if your dog can feel where you are, they're less inclined to look back to check where you are.

....

🐾 Are you remembering to jog backwards a few steps each time you Recall to tap into the chase game and maintain enthusiasm?

....

🐾 Are you being generous with your reinforcement?

....

What was good?

....

....

What could be better?

....

....

What will you do to improve?

....

....

Doggy Diary

Write down all the amazing things you did with your dog this week!

Monday and Tuesday

....

....

....

Wednesday and Thursday

....

....

....

Friday

....

....

....

Saturday and Sunday

....

....

....

WEEK 48
Detection Dog
#4

Challenge: Detection Dog #4

The Target: Test your Detection Dog
handler skills

You're now both going to live the life of a Detection Dog and Handler!

You've triggered the search behaviour by saying 'Find It'; you've taught your dog to indicate on a specific target scent; and you've taught them to search an area in the hope of such a find. So now let's put all of those skills together and start searching for some smugglers!

The Training

1. Rather than the saucepans, put three chairs in a row in a line going away from you. Put the target scent pot on the chair nearest to you and your dog. (If you've a tiny dog, slide the pot under a cushion or attach to a lower part of the chair.) Ask your dog to 'Find It', bring them to the first chair, let them have a good sniff and *as soon as they target the pot with their nose*, say, 'Good' and shower your dog with treats, toys, love, a new bike . . . whatever they desire, they deserve it! Repeat several times so your dog can't wait to get their search on.

2. Leave the target scent pot on the original chair, but move the chair that was originally furthest from them up to the front. Now, the target scent pot should be on the second chair that you **both** search. When your dog indicates onto the target, say, 'Good' and reinforce as before.

3. With the scent pot still on the original chair, now have both of the other chairs at the start of the line. This time, you'll be searching the two dummy chairs before hitting your find.

4. Now add three human helpers. Have one of them sneak the target scent pot into their pocket before all three take a seat on your queue of chairs. Ask your dog to 'Find It' and when they freeze to indicate the contraband in the 'bad' guy's pocket, GO BANANAS What a Team! Hot dogs and cheese for EVERYONE!

Easy Peasy Ponder Points

🐾 Would a lead help you search in a more orderly fashion?

....

🐾 Is your body language helping your dog, or getting in the way?

....

🐾 When indicating, is your dog focused on the scent, or you?

....

🐾 How else can you celebrate a great find?

....

🐾 Rather than all at once, would you be better to introduce one human, then two, then three?

....

🐾 When searching outside, how does the wind direction affect the performance?

....

🐾 Can you transfer your skills to another room? Outside?

....

🐾 How proud are you of your dog right now? Be proud of yourself also. Thanks for doing this with your dog, you're making their life fuller.

....

What was good?

....

What could be better?

....

What will you do to improve?

....

Easy Peasy
Pearl of Wisdom:
THE 'BAD-BEHAVIOUR' BUSTER!

O f course, there's no such thing as 'bad' behaviour from your dog, certainly not as far as they're concerned!

For a dog, it's simply 'behaviour that *works*, and behaviour that doesn't work'.

For you, it's simply 'behaviour you *like*, and behaviour you don't like'. For a **short-term solution** to 'bad behaviour', use good Control & Management: for example, think about leads and doors to ensure the behaviour you *don't like* – such as running off down the street – doesn't *work* for your dog.

For the **long-term solution** to 'bad behaviour', you're going to teach your dog that instead of the unwanted behaviour, there's other more *likeable* and FAR MORE reinforcing behaviours that they can do instead to get exactly what they want.

That way, your dog gets what they want; you get what you want. It's a WIN–WIN!

Here's a Pro Dog Trainer's tip! When I speak to a client, I get them to tell me the behaviours they don't want from their dog (owners are EXPERTS in what they DON'T want their dog to do!).

I get a piece of paper and write all of those behaviours in the left-hand column; in the middle column, I write the owner's answers to my question, 'What behaviour would you like instead?' I save the right-hand column so the owner can decide how they'd like to reinforce the more likeable behaviour.

Have a look at the table below to explain this idea a little more. I've listed a few just to get you started. Again, free of charge.

What other unwanted behaviours could you eliminate by reinforcing a more likeable behaviour in its place?

UNWANTED BEHAVIOUR	MORE LIKEABLE BEHAVIOUR	REINFORCED BY...
Jumping up at visitors	Sit	Visitors only saying, 'Hello' when your dog sits.
Pulling on the lead to play with other dogs	Slack lead	Releasing your dog with a 'Go play' when they turn to look at you.
Peeing on the carpet!	Peeing in the garden	Raining treats upon your dog when they toilet outside.

WEEK 49
The Emergency Drop #4

Challenge: The Emergency Drop #4

The Target: Role Play

You've *layered* all of the important stages so now your dog will let go of any item during training when you say, 'Drop'. The final cherry on the cake is for you to now create a few real-life scenarios where a Drop may be a life-saver. Try the steps that follow and if any seem a little sticky, lower the criteria a little by using a more boring item, or practising a few easier versions of the exercise first, before raising the bar. There's no such thing as a failure, only feedback so you can design your next attempt!

For the first role-play attempt opposite, *try* and act normal. *'Dum-de-dum, nothing going on here . . .'* you know what I mean, like when you drop a massive tray of drinks at the pub but you try to style it out as you tip-toe out of the pub, under the door, whistling . . .

The Training

1. Fuss around your kitchen like you're preparing a banquet. *Accidentally* (winks to audience) knock a tennis ball off the worktop, then as soon as your dog picks it up say, 'Drop' and place a bounty of treats by your feet for them to enjoy.

2. Throw a toy for your dog in the garden, then as they run back to you with it in their mouth shout, 'Drop' and as they spit the toy, double treats: one at your feet, the second thrown.

3. At the park, pull out your tea-towel toy and have a good game of ragging together. Mid-play, freeze the toy in your hands, say, 'Drop' and as soon as your dog lets go, say, 'Good' and reinforce by continuing the game.

Easy Peasy Ponder Points

🐾 How do arousal levels affect your dog's Drop performance?

....

....

....

🐾 List 5 place indoors and 5 places outdoors you can practise:

1. .... 1. ....
2. .... 2. ....
3. .... 3. ....
4. .... 4. ....
5. .... 5. ....

🐾 Before teaching this skill, when did you ever wish your dog already knew Drop?

....

....

....

What was good?

....

....

....

....

What could be better?

....

....

....

....

What will you do to improve?

....

....

....

....

Doggy Diary

Write down all the amazing things you did with your dog this week!

Monday and Tuesday

....

....

....

Wednesday and Thursday

....

....

....

Friday

....

....

....

Saturday and Sunday

....

....

....

WEEK 50
Hit The Brakes
#4

Challenge: Hit The Brakes #4

The Target: Changing the context, maintaining the behaviour

You've now completed all of the difficult yards to teach your dog to Hit the Brakes. All that's left now is to practise in as many different environments and contexts as you can to make the behaviour as reliable and robust as possible. The cue, the body language, the behaviour and reinforcement will all remain the same; it's just the 'picture' where the exercise is being performed that will change . . .

The Training

- Practise with your dog running towards you
- Practise with your dog running away from you
- Practise with your dog up close to you
- Practise when they're playing with another dog (good luck!)

Remember to pay well, don't be too greedy with your expectations and keep each session enjoyable.

Easy Peasy Ponder Points

🐾 What variable seemed most tricky?

....

🐾 How can you lower the criteria to build on success?

....

🐾 What else could you throw to your dog for stopping?
(a party perhaps!)

....

What was good?

....

What could be better?

....

What will you do to improve?

....

Doggy Diary

Write down all the amazing things you did with your dog this week!

Monday and Tuesday

....

....

....

Wednesday and Thursday

....

....

....

Friday

....

....

....

Saturday and Sunday

....

....

....

WEEK 51
Say Your Prayers
#4

Challenge: Say Your Prayers #4

The Target: Join Hands In Prayer!

To really funk up this exercise, let's get a bit more hands-on! You're going to kneel down next to your dog then offer your arm out for them to 'paws-up' onto, in order to say their prayers. Good luck if you've got a Great Dane or St Bernard!

The Training

1. Kneel next to your dog with them facing the platform. Put your left arm out to your side and rest it along the platform's edge, nearest to your dog.

2. With your right arm, lure your dog's two front feet up onto your own arm with the cue of 'Target', then when your dog's feet are in position on your arm, say, 'Good' and treat your dog.

3. Again, with your arm across the platform, cue your dog to 'Target', lure their feet onto your arm and then with a treat, lure your dog's head down to rest their chin on your forearm. Say 'Good' and reinforce with several individual treats as they maintain their 'praying' position.

4. Final step is to brace yourself, remove the platform, kneel with outstretched arm and cue your dog to 'Target' to hop up to your arm, then 'Prayers' to drop their head (solemnly).

Easy Peasy Ponder Points

🐾 Would it help to rest your hand on the platform as
you encourage your dog to target your arm?

....

🐾 Try the opposite hand, what differences do you notice?

....

🐾 List 5 locations you can practise 'Say Your Prayers'
this week:

1. ....
2. ....
3. ....
4. ....
5. ....

🐾 List 5 activities that two-feet-on-a-target could assist
with. (I'll start you off with Grooming and Ear
Cleaning!):

1. Grooming and ear cleaning
2. ....
3. ....
4. ....
5. ....

What was good?

....

....

....

....

What could be better?

....

....

....

....

What will you do to improve?

....

....

....

....

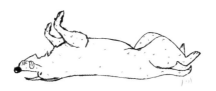

Doggy Diary

Write down all the amazing things you did with your dog this week!

Monday and Tuesday

....

....

....

Wednesday and Thursday

....

....

....

Friday

....

....

....

Saturday and Sunday

....

....

....

WEEK 52

Rock Around
The Clock #4

Challenge: Rock Around The Clock #4

The Target: The big one!

Remember that bet we had earlier about your dog Recalling to you by stepping over the ham? We can't put it off any longer . . .

The Training

1. With your dog in a Sit at 6 o'clock, place a treat on the bowl in the centre of the clock face and step over to 10 o'clock. When your dog looks to you, Recall, Hand Touch, 'Good!' TREAT!

2. . . . as above, but rather than returning to '10' after placing the treat, return to 11 o'clock . . .

3. Get 5 out of 5 consistently . . . then let's do the BIG one . . .

4. With your dog in a Sit at 6 o'clock, place a SLICE OF HAM on the bowl in the centre of the clock face and step over to 12 o'clock.

5. You should be now facing your dog, with the slice of ham directly between the two of you . . . be still my beating heart . . . I can hardly take the tension!

6. Call your dog . . .

(*Now, when the inevitable movie is made about your Around-the-Clock training, this is where the screen silently fades to black and the credits begin to roll, leaving the packed cinema wide-eyed and open-mouthed.*)

WHEN your dog comes to you, wipe a solitary tear from your eye, get your Hand Touch and run back with your dog to help them celebrate National Ham Day!

You did it!

Easy Peasy Ponder Points

🐾 List 3 benefits you can now enjoy due to successfully improving your dog's Sit, Eye Contact, Recall and Touch, in the face of HUGE temptation:

1. ....

2. ....

3. ....

🐾 List 3 different locations you can practise your Around The Clock:

1. ....

2. ....

3. ....

🐾 What differences do you notice in your dog's performance when you make the clock face smaller?

....

🐾 What differences do you notice in your dog's performance when you make the clock face larger?

....

This isn't so much an EASY PEASY PONDER POINT, just an opportunity for me to say: Well done! *Thank you for all of your efforts to improve your dog's quality of life. You Rock!*

What was good?

....

....

What could be better?

....

....

What will you do to improve?

....

....

BON VOYAGE

S o that's it, we're done! *

Thanks so much for the time and effort you put into your dog and your training.

* Don't think that's it finished forever though!

Training your dog is always a work-in-progress and standards never stay the same.

Keep going with your training, revisit these pages as a 'refresher' course every now and then and continue to be the best advocate for your dog.

It'll be interesting to see the difference in your Ponder Point reflections as time progresses. Be warned, I do perform random spot checks, so if the doorbell goes and you pick up on the slight aroma of liver cake in the hallway, your Diary better be up to date.

First and foremost enjoy your time with your dog, make sure they enjoy every second with you and keep up the good work!

Onwards!